D0849197

# the Minister and Grief

# the Minister and Grief

ROBERT W. BAILEY

HAWTHORN BOOKS, INC.
*W. Clement Stone, Publisher*
NEW YORK

# Contents

# Preface

Throughout my ministry, I have been impressed by the fact that the minister is offered little insight into dealing with dying, death, and grief in a personal manner. That is not to say there is a shortage of books containing sermons and poems for funerals. But there is little helpful material for a minister who earnestly desires to relate with integrity and support to a bereaved family.

The purpose of this volume is to chart a course that has proved helpful for me. I seek to share it because my colleagues—clergymen and funeral directors alike—have suggested that this approach has been an aid to them.

I also feel this book will be appreciated by lay Christians who seek a Christian view of death, who desire to minister more effectively to dying and bereaved persons, and who would like to develop solid concepts for planning a Christian funeral for family members or for themselves.

The initial chapter states an attitude church members need to develop toward life and death. This chapter grew out of several sermons I have preached to my parishioners.

The second chapter treats the minister's feelings about death. I am convinced that if a minister is to have an effective ministry to a bereaved family, he must have had the prior experience of identifying and dealing with his own feelings about death.

The third chapter describes the reactions and needs of dying persons. I also suggest some ways of strengthening the ministry both to the dying and to his family.

The next chapter gives a rationale for a Christian funeral. Some insights will help a church to plan a well-designed order of worship rather than merely following a cultural tradition through mere habit.

The fifth chapter lists some practical steps to take when death occurs. While running the risk of appearing mundane, I feel it is important to have a plan of response that one can follow when death takes place.

The sixth chapter portrays an example of my ministry to a bereaved family. Rather than limiting suggestions to the funeral service, I trace some helpful facets of ministry to the family before, during, and after the funeral.

The seventh chapter describes concepts to develop in grief counseling following the funeral. Prefaced with a summary of types of grief and stages of grief, there are some practical suggestions for developing a stronger grief ministry.

The final chapter offers some resources for funerals. Since there is no intent that this be another "funeral manual," the material is not designed for a person to read from the pulpit during a funeral. However, care has been taken to suggest helpful concepts of liturgy and content for funerals.

Following a brief conclusion, a sample funeral appears in the appendix.

Innumerable families have found help in reading Edgar N. Jackson's little book, *You and Your Grief*. My hope is that ministers may receive that kind of help and inspiration from this book. If this is true, perhaps the ministry during grief will be more lasting and therapeutic.

# the Minister and Grief

# 1
# Facing Life and Death

Autumn is for most of us a beautiful season—though for some it is depressing. The latter look at the death of leaves, flowers, and grass and feel the coming of winter as an unwelcome reminder of their own human frailties and the uncertainty of life. As a college student, I once made a trip with five friends. While we traveled through the mountains of east Tennessee, we observed and began to talk about the advent of autumn. Four of the students expressed their dismay during autumn and the winter that followed. They said it depressed them to see the lifeless gloom. I will never forget what the fifth person said—that she had always enjoyed fall and winter, for this time of year reminded her of the solitude and rest needed by all of nature before the coming of new growth and new life.

If we were to devise some measuring tool, I rather expect the response of my fellow students would hold up in society as a whole. Most of us are unprepared and unwilling to talk about, to accept, or to face the reality of death. The German preacher-theologian, Helmut Thielicke, pinpointed this issue when he wrote: "Every attempt to get at the meaning of life must inevitably face the question of death."[1]

When we fail to deal with death, we also fail to come to grips with life. Edgar N. Jackson has written a number of books on death and grief. In one he wrote: "I have seen people who have lost their will to live because they were so overwhelmed by a fear of death. I have seen people become impotent in the face of important life crises because their anxiety possessed them so completely that their fear of death made them afraid to live."[2]

Because of the rising interest in the subject of life and death, the multiple dimensions of the topic, and the need for greater perception and response to anxious persons, it is important to examine some of the common outlooks on life and death.

## OUTLOOKS ON LIFE AND DEATH

Philosophers have found death an acceptable part of the natural rhythm of life, like the ebb and flow of the tide. However, in today's society the ways in which people face or fail to face life and death are myriad. Corpses are made to appear still alive. Cemeteries are called memorial gardens. Sickness is confined to hospitals. The aged are placed in institutions. Even the sounds of birth are kept out of the range of hearing. Attempts to ignore these human levels of awareness defy life itself. A review of the varied feelings people have about life and death might aid in understanding modern man. Recognizing that there are many possible approaches in giving a summary description, I have chosen the categories of defiance, denial, anxiety, emptiness, melo-drama, and tragedy.

*Defiance.* For many centuries, and particularly the last one, a common response to life and death has been one of defiance. This concept is based on the Greek philosophy that the divine soul of man is imprisoned within an evil body. The ultimate goal is to free the soul from the sinful body. Therefore life here is just a necessary stage, a time of testing, a temporary preparation for the real existence of the soul beyond this earth. Rather than fear or begrudge death, it is a welcomed companion. After all, while on this earth you are but a wayfaring stranger on your way to a better place. Other than an opportunity to prepare for future life, existence on this earth has no meaning.

It is interesting to note in light of the popularity of this outlook that it has no biblical basis. However, due to the brevity and uncertainty of life on the frontier, this concept received wide acceptance in past generations. While today we are saturated with the possibilities of abundant life, contemporary Americans have become calloused toward the potential of life as well as the reality of death. Life is still frequently considered as just a necessary evil. It is something to be endured until the day when we can die and go to heaven. Songs and theology from the past are combined with new music and concepts to make this outlook one still to be reckoned with in the last quarter of the twentieth century.

*Denial.* Another common response to death is to deny that it is a possibility for yourself. Frequently when persons refer to death, they do not speak of it in terms of "my" death but only when "one" dies or when "they" die. There are many solemn reminders of death all about us—cemeteries, accidents, wars, auto fatalities, and famine. Still many try to deny death as a reality for themselves. There is a ready identification with the star of the television series of several years ago, "The Immortal." Because of his unique blood, he could not die. His body repaired faster than it was hurt. We, too, feel we can somehow conquer death and live forever. By narrowly avoiding death in a car wreck or by escaping death on a battlefield, we may feel immune to death. Or it may be that, through the accomplishments of medical science, we feel we will escape death through a personally granted state of immortality.

There has been such a rapid advancement of medical science that people have been encouraged to deny death. After all, when we get sick, all we have to do is to go to the doctor in order to be made well! And if our condition appears to be terminal, the expectation is that a new discovery on the horizon can still eliminate death. One extreme shape this outlook has taken is the development of cryonics. I have heard people say, with happiness and favor, that if and when they contracted a terminal illness for which there was no known cure, they wanted to be frozen until a cure could be discovered. Then they wanted to be thawed, cured, and sent on their way to a happy state of immortality on earth!

Contemporary American custom considers it somehow improper for us to mention death, even at funerals! Almost everything we do and say is a facade or denial of death. Instead of actually using the word "dead," we use phrases such as "expired," "passed away," "gone to his reward," "terminated," "dropped off," "asleep," "departed," "no longer with us," "left," or "passed on." Professionals, including ministers and medical personnel, are often reluctant to disclose that death is impending. Frequently they will avoid contact with the dying. They do so because they cannot come to grips with their lack of power over death and because they are reminded of their own inevitable death. Refusal to be near—or to be honest with—a dying person is simply a form of denying death. One reason we grieve when a person dies is that we realize that we, too, will die—and we do not want to admit it!

*Anxiety.* The fear of death, when pushed out of the conscious mind, creates anxiety and personal disorders. More than one person in the field of psychiatry has suggested that the professionals need to get their heads together before society becomes so terrified by death that it destroys itself.

Rollo May has developed an interesting theory through his extensive psychiatric work. He concludes that the psychic problems of contemporary man are not rooted in sexual repression as Freud believed. Rather, May feels that anxiety about death is the primary problem, and preoccupation with sex is only a symptom. Potency in sex is equated with life, and diminishing sexual virility is equated with death. The use and misuse of sex are attempts to hide the presence of death. If we could lay aside our obsession with sex, we would then see that we must die!

Anxiety about death raises its head in other forms. The use of drugs is often tied to the desire to be rid of the frustrations and anxieties of this life—to squeeze eternity into the now. Violence might be viewed as a method of striking at death before it strikes at us. The national grief over a figure like President John F. Kennedy was tied in with the anxiety over the fact that if a hero can die, then we, too, can.

Another phase of anxiety about death was detected by a psychiatrist who wrote: "Death is simply a special example of many situations common to human life which offer people an unusual opportunity for growth. . . . The fear of death is simply the fear of growing. . . ."[3]

Facing growth in life or death causes bitterness and fear in us, for both processes involve personal loss. When change is included in an experience, we face the possibility of internalizing something new and the reality of giving up something old. We might seek to avoid growth by using masks or roles to deceive both ourselves and others. We rationalize and defend what we are and do as long as we can. But ultimately we must deal with the fact that death forces us to distinguish between the false and the real in life and in ourselves.

*Emptiness.* In the late sixties the popular singer, Peggy Lee, sang a very intriguing and haunting song entitled, "Is That All There Is?" I feel it expresses the attitude of many who are trying to cope with a sense of emptiness regarding life and death.

The song describes the singer's reaction of disappointment on various occasions in her life—when her house burned, when she first saw a circus, when her lover left her. After each of these she felt a sense of emptiness and disappointment, for these things were not all she had anticipated them to be. Acknowledging her sense of futility, her friends asked why she did not end her life. Her reply was that she was not prepared for what to her would be the final disappointment, because she knew that even when she faced death, she would still feel "Is that all there is?"[4]

This song is a sad indictment of many people across our land. There are those who have tried everything and still found something lacking—excitement, fulfillment, or purpose. Both life and death seem little more than an empty disappointment. After being hurt or disappointed once, many people seem to face the rest of life in a fatalistic, indifferent, lifeless manner. Some people try to fill the loneliness and meaninglessness of their lives with everything from sex, possessions, work, leisure, marriage, family, piety, hopes, and positive thinking to religious activism. But none of these things dissolves the emptiness within. For those who are pursuing happiness, fruitless though their efforts may be, death is feared as an interruption of their quest.

*Melodrama.* Almost every American views life as a time to be happy. In a lecture entitled. "Grief as a Question for the Christian Faith," Dr. William Spong of the Episcopal Seminary in Austin, Texas, suggested two ways of viewing your life from birth to death. One is as a melodrama, which represents the possibility of intervention. The other is as a tragedy, which represents no possibility of intervention. The outlook of the melodrama is that everybody ought to be happy and joyful. This means that if we have intermittent moments of being unhappy—through grief, hurt, loss, or trauma—they are violations of the normal human experience. Therefore we can wrestle tragic experiences back into happy ones, often with such cliches as: "You may not know today what good will come from this, but . . ." The overview of melodrama cannot tolerate tragedy, so we try to swing everything quickly back to joy. Whatever this situation, we feel that our rescuer will arrive just in time to save us.

If we hold this view, we cannot say we will die. It would be a violation of the norm to admit our own death. We would respond like the ninety-four-year-old who told an inquirer why he was planting a tree. He said he lived as though he would never die. In the back of our minds we hold onto the dream that the hero on the white horse, the doctor with unlimited skills, the new lifesaving invention, the water from the fountain of youth will come to us just in time to assure our continued happiness and to prevent our ever dying.

*Tragedy.* The other life continuum Spong described was tragedy. Rooted in Greek tragedy, everyone knows the conclusion to this outlook on life. There is no possibility for intervention. The destiny of the hero is known. There is no hope. And yet this very fact makes for rest and peace. We can honestly shout and get our frustrations off our chests because we know we will die.

Zorba the Greek epitomized the tragic view of life when he declared his belief that life is what a person does while he is waiting to die. Indeed, life is all of the time gone by. Contrary to the old tree planter, Zorba was spontaneously alive, saying he lived as though he would die any minute. And therefore he was free. He was not hiding from his humanness, his finiteness, or his inevitable death.

By tragedy I do not mean to infer that everything is bad.

Accepting tragedy means that in life we recognize that there will be pain, suffering, unexpected trauma, grief, and ultimately death. This is the reality of life. Tragedy is the norm. And from this outlook Zorba's words can sound joyful. His belief can be an affirmation of freedom if we accept life's qualities of destiny and limitation. We cannot live without dying!

The tragic times of life are interrupted by moments of joy, which we can reach out and enjoy. We can celebrate and share these moments with others because we know they do not happen all the time. But it is hard to celebrate happiness with one who tries to make every experience of every day a happy one. There is the tragic element of life.

## EXPECTATION OF GOD

Our expectation of God colors how we face life and death. From the melodramatic view of life, God seems to be the keeper of the joy gate. There are certain amounts of happiness for the faithful, praying Christians and those who do good works. But a dying person cannot live with this concept of God!

If we do not expect God to deliver us from all pain, suffering, and death, there are other false images of God in death, such as: "God loved him so much he wanted him to come home." "It was his time." "It was a tragedy that maybe will cause someone to become a Christian."

These views of God are ultimately unacceptable. They make of God something other than a loving being. While God can take evil situations and bring good out of them, he does not use evil means to achieve good ends. Frequently people fail to make this distinction. Perhaps the translation of Rom. 8:28 (AV) has attributed to this misunderstanding in the last three centuries. The Greek is reflected in more recent translations, which read, "For we know that in all things God works for good with those who love him, those whom he has called according to his purpose." (TEV)

The AV reads: "And we know that all things work together for good to them that love God, to them who are called according to his purpose."

God can help his followers to salvage something from tragedy, but from my interpretation of the Scriptures, he does not create a tragedy in order to have something to salvage!

In this life God does not seek to shield us from pain, suffering, and death. He does seek to enable us to become genuine disciples of Christ. If we are open to the possibility, we can learn obedience to Christ in the midst of our suffering. Viktor Frankl, the German Christian who underwent persecution in the Nazi prison camps, has declared that there are three kinds of values. One is achieving, or producing something to meet man's needs. A second is experiencing, or appreciating truth, beauty, and goodness. The third is suffering, or coming to terms with one's humanness. Life, suffering, and death all have meaning.

In the summer of 1973 I read with literal horror about the young couple who allowed their eleven-year-old son to die in a diabetic coma after they threw away his insulin. They first claimed he had been cured by a faith healer. When he died they asserted God would raise him from the grave four days later. The father admitted he was disappointed when the fourth day came and passed, but he still thought something would happen. What did occur was that these sick, confused parents, who had such an unrealistic expectation of God, now face manslaughter charges for what they did to their son.

Our choices in the face of death are bitterness toward God and life, and despair in life's tragedies, or hope that God's work is not yet complete. C. S. Lewis, a profound thinker who became a Christian as an adult, married Joy Davidman, another adult convert, late in life. Not many years after their blissful, fulfilling marriage, Lewis had to watch his wife die an agonizing death of cancer. In his book, *A Grief Observed,* he reveals how depressed he was with his religion. He thought there were resources available to make things different, but he felt nothing was happening. It was some time before he came to realize that his problem lay not in God's failure, but in himself, C.S. Lewis! His expectations of life and death were unreal.[5]

Man cannot manipulate God to act through professed faith. As one physician was reported to have said, there is nothing worse about a God who would allow one child to die of leukemia than a God who would heal it—and then ignore the thousands who go unhealed! Thus we can believe in spiritual healing, but only so long as that healing includes death. We do know that out of his tragic death on the Cross, God in his mystery did bring forth life, light, and hope for all mankind. While we cannot fathom the mysteries of life and death, we know that God has not forsaken us, and we know that in his power there is ultimate victory over death. After my former minister, John R. Claypool, had watched helplessly as his daughter was dying with leukemia, Carlyle Marney wrote to him: "I fall back on the idea that God has a lot to give an account for."[6] And we can trust that God will. Dr. Marney is not challenging or blaspheming God. He is giving an affirmation of what God can and will do.

## An Approach to a Christian View of Life and Death

Where can we go to get the strength to face life and death? We cannot find it by looking at the tragedies of the past and asking why. Job finally thrust aside the so-called friends who had tried to explain life solely by an intellectual analysis of why things happen as they do. When Job was encountered by

God in the whirlwind, he came to realize what was of ultimate importance. He could not fathom the mystery of why things happened, but he could sense God's presence through all of his experiences. For God to have explained everything to Job would be like trying to explain Einstein's theory of relativity to a small-necked crab! Job asked why he had suffered. He learned that everything he had was a gift from God, and he sensed that God did not forsake him. As one writer expressed this truth: "Even covered with sores and ashes, he looks oddly like a man who has asked for a crust and been given the whole loaf."[7]

Job got not what he asked for, but he got what he needed the most—the companionship of God! He gives himself as the answer to our perplexities of life.

Isaiah pointed out to us the redeeming God who offers his strength to all those who wait for him, to those who are open to and dependent upon him. On the basis of his promises, God sometimes comes to us with wings like eagles. Other times God gives energy for activism, the "thyroid of the spirit," which motivates men to "problem-solving activity." God also offers the gift of endurance, the strength to walk and not faint. (Isa. 40:28–31) In every instance, God does not abandon us.

After Dr. Claypool had sat helplessly by his ten-year-old daughter's bedside for two weeks, a friend asked if God really made any difference at a time like that. Dr. Claypool responded that he did—not with soaring ecstasy or energetic activism but with quiet endurance God came to him and undergirded him. We need to be open and responsive to God at all three levels. We need not declare that if there is no ecstasy or some solution of activism God is not with us. Sometimes God's best, his only gift, is the strength of endurance.[8]

What poses a greater fear or evil than physical death itself is the absence of life while we are living. In her book,

*Peoplemaking,* Virginia Satir writes: "Many people fear death so much that they die a little every day, and the rest of the time they are trying to avoid dying so they really die before they ever had a chance to live."[9]

Those who grieve at the falling autumn leaves have forgotten about the exciting new growth the spring will bring. More than one person has connected anxiety about death with anxiety about "being-in-the world" itself. Death, however, means more than biological extinction. Living can be a type of death. Real death is separation from God, degeneration of character, unresolved conflicts with others, lack of self-identity, or the inability to affirm oneself as a person of worth. As one person described this reality: "Death is the contemporaneous power abrasively addressing every man at his own existence with the word that he is not only eventually and finally, but even now and already, estranged, separated, alienated, lost in his relationships with, at once, everybody and everything else and—what is, in a way, much worse—his very own self. Death means loss of identity."[10]

Viewed in proper perspective, life and death can be affirmed and embraced. A meeting has a beginning and an ending. A drama has the first curtain and the final curtain. An experience of corporate worship has a call to worship and a benediction. The adjournment, the benediction, is literally and figuratively a blessing. I thank God that he does not make us go on living through endless suffering and deterioration in this physical body. I am glad I can acknowledge that this body, which is made of dust, will not have to support me for hundreds or thousands of years.

At a homecoming in a church from which my family had moved some ten years before, a number of families invited us to come visit them. Several of them told us they had moved to a new house. One spoke a profound truth when he said their old house had decayed so much that it was no longer a comfortable place in which to live. Therefore they built a new house on the farm and moved out of the old one into the new one. Their family was still intact, and they were so much more comfortable and happy now. God makes that provision for us. We do not have to remain in a decayed body. We can move into a new residence, a new, completed fellowship with God in Christ Jesus.

Death is what we have in common with each other and all of creation. Death is equal for us all. I feel our reluctance to embrace life and death is due to our failure to respond fully to God's will in Christ to "come to him," to lose our life for the sake of Christ and his good news. (Matt. 11:28–30; Mark 8:35) This is why we fear both death at the end of life and a lifeless existence while we are on this earth. Loneliness is overcome through submission to Christ, who, in his subjection to death, took the dread out of loneliness. God's initiative through Christ affirms our creation and gives us new life. We are never alone! We are free in the life given us by God. We can love ourselves, we can love others, even as we love and are loved by God. We do not have to fear rejection, failure to succeed or to accomplish. We can be whole! Indeed, we can enjoy God, participating in our work and leisure in a way that is virtually indistinguishable from our worship. We can enjoy God's love for us and everyone, even those who do not yet enjoy God's love.

At death we are in actual fact at our end, but our history with God does not stop, since we are redeemed by Christ. (Rom. 8:35–39) God is there to unravel the final mystery. Even more, when we believe in Christ, we have already passed from death into life. (John 5:24; 1 John 3:14) Thus death has lost its killing power. We who are in fellowship with Christ need be enslaved to the fear of death no longer, neither should we allow the false gods of death to separate us from God. While death is not removed, it is rendered impotent. Because of our relationship to God, we can die in peace.

Not long ago a lady in her eighties, who has a terminal heart condition, shared with me these words of wisdom she had read. This could inspire an outlook for facing life and death: "I am not afraid of tomorrow for I have seen yesterday and I love today!"

The good news for us who are in Christ is that God has not offered us pie-in-the-sky-by-and-by. He has offered us a complete gift—eternal life that begins now and knows no end. God has promised never to leave us. Indeed, Christ told his disciples that their sense of the presence of God would be heightened, not lessened, while he was physically absent and the Holy Spirit was felt in their midst. (John 14:25–27) God does not forsake us in life, neither does he forsake us beyond life.

When our son, Kevin, was younger, my wife and I had explained to him about the needs of people, particularly those who live alone. We told him that sometimes they may be lonely, but they will never be alone, for God will be with them. One day as I was going to visit a sick relative of one of his little friends, I told my son the purpose of the visit. He responded by asking me to tell her that God loves her and that she might be lonely in the hospital, but that she would not be alone, for God would be with her! The Word that God loves us, that we cannot go from his presence—this is the Word we have been searching to hear! But realize Jesus said it is only through a childlike faith, not childish but childlike faith in him that our lives can be made whole. (Mark 10:14–15)

I thank God that since I have lived yesterday in his presence, and I love living today with him, I am not afraid of tomorrow with him. With the prospect of a martyr's death staring him in the face, Paul was able to declare: "I have fought the good fight, I have finished the race, I have kept the faith. Henceforth there is laid up for me the crown of righteousness, which the Lord, the righteous judge, will award to me on that Day, and not only to me but also to all who have loved his appearing." (2 Tim. 4:7–8 RSV)

Most of us are people who, unlike Paul, have not genuinely come to grips with life or death. At the conclusion of his book, Edgar N. Jackson wrote: "Perhaps when the history of this era is written, it will be pointed out that this was the age of the great anxiety, when the inability of people to face life and death produced a crippling philosophy of life. Wise in science, rich in things, yet our time is fractured at the point of the meaning of life itself because the fear of death has become so irrational."[11]

Many of us are stumbling through life with this irrational outlook. We are facing life in a glib, meaningless manner, thinking one day we will take up the Cross of Christ and bear his yoke. But not now! The saddest part about failing to face death is that we also fail to face life. When the day of our death comes and we ultimately realize life has not been lived fully, it will be too late for us to know any difference in the living of life. If we are going to escape the fear of death, we must escape the meaninglessness of life now. Most often the art of living and dying with meaning is gained at the beginning of life instead of at the end. If we are going to be able to face death, we must also be able to face and live life. The poet, Stephen Vincent Benét, wrote:

> "Life is not lost by dying! Life is lost
> Minute by minute, day by dragging day,
> In all the thousand, small, uncaring ways."[12]

Life is not found just in talking, but in living. Death comes even in life when we refuse to exercise the life God gave us, when we decline to live beyond the confines of mere existence. We are to be freed of the anxiety over life and death when we know we are secure in the hands of God. When we live life we can die death, all with dependence on and commitment to God, the author and finisher of the mystery of life and death. There is more than death for the person who is related to

17

God in Christ. There is strong word of hope we need to resound to replace the futility in life: "There was a time when Spain stamped on her coins the Pillars of Hercules and underneath them the inscription, *Ne Plus Ultra*, meaning, 'No More Beyond.' That is what many people say when they come to the end of life—'No more beyond; nothing on the other side of the blank wall of death;' and if the end of life is nothing, then life itself, the preface to that end, is nothing. But the picture can change and sometimes does change. Columbus discovered a new world far beyond the Pillars of Hercules, so the Spanish government deleted the *ne* and left the *plus ultra*, meaning 'More beyond.' One thing can save life from futility—hope that there is more beyond, hope that the lives, the loves, and the labours begun in time do not end in time but find their fulfilment in eternity."[13]

Last year our little daughter, Courtney, saw the picture of her grandparents. When she recognized her grandmother she exclaimed with excitement, "Nana!" Kevin then assumed the role of his little sister's teacher as he pointed to the man in the picture and told her he was her grandfather and he had gone to live with God. Kevin suddenly turned to me and asked as the thought came to him for the first time: "Daddy, how does God get someone to heaven?"

I responded as simply as I could, telling him we cannot understand all God does, but we know that God loves us and takes those who love him to live with him when they die. With a smile Kevin then added: "That just shows us how much God loves us—and Jesus loves us, too—because God does things for us we don't understand."

When we can affirm this truth, expressed in childlike faith, then we can face both life and death!

# 2
# The Minister's Attitude toward Death

There is almost a preoccupation with death and dying in contemporary news, television programs, school electives, and the printed word. Frequently the spokesmen not only are not ministers but are not even Christians. To me this is a sad indictment on the silence of the Christian ministry on this subject of grave concern. I feel it is important for contemporary ministers to decide why there is real reluctance to speak honestly about death.

A prior need is for the minister to face his own feelings, including understanding why he is a minister. Both studies and personal observation verify that some men enter the vocation of clergyman for the security and acceptance of God and others. Much of what some ministers have done amounts to little more than an attempt to comfort themselves. A minister may hide his feelings, his fears, his anxieties about life and death by offering polite, saccharine generalizations about death. In the process of protecting himself, he ignores the reality of the actual loss and hurt involved in the experience of dying or the grief of the loved ones.

When a minister comes to grips with his own sense of impending death and his attitude toward grief, he still cannot work out a system of helping others painlessly through their experiences. There is no easy way! And the minister who attempts to provide a prefabricated, smooth route does a disservice both to his parishioners and to himself.

## THE STRUGGLE TO INTERPRET LIFE AND DEATH

As more than one person has already pointed out, it is a bit naïve to assume the role of an authority on the matter of death. After all, normally one becomes an authority due to his experience with the subject. Like everyone else who is living and writing, I have not experienced death! However, I feel it might be helpful for me to attempt to describe my own struggle to interpret life and death.

During my first year of ministry in a church of more than 1,000 members, I was called upon numerous times to minister to families who had had a death in the family. As I moved among people I had not had the opportunity to know before, I longed for the time to interpret prior to the hour of death that for those who are in Christ, there is more than death. While death does come to all of us, death is not all there is. This thought never left my mind during those early months of ministry in this parish. However, it was the reading of a book entitled *On Death and Dying* by Elizabeth Kübler-Ross[1] that my thoughts and feelings crystallized. The author, a psychiatrist in a Chicago hospital, worked with divinity students at the Chicago Theological Seminary. Her book deals with the interviews and reactions to the interviews of some two hundred persons who were hospitalized with terminal illnesses.

I suppose an idea from her book spurred me to deal with this subject of death and grief. The crucial point for me was not the interchange with the patients. I was indicted by her introductory statement about death. She said that for all of us, in our unconscious minds, death is never possible in regard to ourselves. If your life, if my life, has to come to an end, the ending is always blamed on malicious intervention from the "outside," whether by evil or by God. In other words, your unconscious being only conceives of your death as being killed. We do not think of dying a natural death, dying from an illness, or dying of old age. Death, for most people, is a bad act, an evil, frightening experience.

At first I did not want to agree with her evaluation. But then I had to admit that my personal feeling was honestly quite similar to what she had said. Thoughts about my death have seemed to focus on an evil intervention in life rather than a completion to life. However, as I searched God's Word, I came often to the dynamic statements of the Apostle Paul. Intellectually, I began to be able to affirm that death is not all there is. There is something more, something better in the completion of life, for therein we know the full and complete fellowship with God in Christ and all the host of Christians. Therefore, I do not have to deny the reality of death.

Paul helped me to avoid denying and defying death. He said that for him living was being in Christ, and in death that fellowship with Christ would then be complete. On the one hand he said that it would be better for him to go on and die and be with Christ. But, on the other hand, he recognized it was more important for him to remain alive to accomplish the tasks Christ had set for him.

Certainly Paul accepted death as a conclusion to life and as a means of full fellowship with Christ. And he also accepted the life of the disciple with all of its demands and responsibilities of service, ministry, proclamation, teaching, and fellowship. Thus, he was not ready to try to escape from this life, nor was he prepared to avoid or deny death. It was at this conclusion that I began to have a more personal view of death as a

Christian. Paul gave me assurance in what I have come to consider the basic thrust of his writing about death:

> None of us lives to himself,
> and none of us dies to himself.
> And if we live, we live to the Lord,
> And if we die, we die to the Lord;
> So then, *whether we live or whether we die,*
> *We are the Lord's!* [emphasis is mine]
> For to this end Christ died and lived again,
> That he might be Lord both of the dead and of the living.
> (Rom. 14:7–9 RSV)

It was through the involved process of thinking and feeling I experienced that I concluded a person cannot have a proper Christian view of death until he has a proper Christian view of life. Or, more pointedly, a person can only see that there is more in life or in death if he is a Christian, but we Christians have a lot to learn! One who fears death cannot truly live. A person cannot really begin to live until he accepts that death is part of life. In his book, *The Common Ventures of Life,* Elton Trueblood wrote: "It is desirable that, as honest men and women, we should face squarely this transcendent fact of death. We are not living wisely or well unless we recognize that whatever we prize most we hold by a slender thread which may, at any moment, be broken. Though it is possible to face this in such a way that our present lives are glorified and our future tragedies made more endurable, the sad fact is that many try to escape the inevitable event and consequently face it suddenly without preparation."[2]

None of us can ever understand all about death—why it comes when it does, or what lies beyond it. But this is not my task anyway! My task is to live and work while it is yet day, and trust that when night comes my same God is Lord of the night just as he is of the day. This is what the Psalmist was testifying of when again and again he wrote of the strength to be found in the Lord in trouble as well as in joy: "God is our refuge and strength, a very present help in trouble. Therefore we will not fear," in life or in death, when we are aware that God is our God, that "The Lord of hosts is with us; the God of Jacob is our refuge." (Ps. 46:1, 11 RSV)

## DEALING WITH OUR OWN FEELINGS

I have observed that many ministers seem to feel immune to death. I can say this since I have been among that number. I am not referring solely to the speed with which the stereotyped minister drives, though this may be a symptom of his defiance of death. I do not mean that he takes critical risks in visiting ill persons. I am simply saying that a minister, like the vast majority of people, sees death only as that which comes to others. I sense that I did not stand alone in the ranks of the clergy when I viewed my death as an outside intervention instead of a natural part of my life.

As I described the various outlooks on death in the preceding chapter, I feel that almost without exception every contemporary minister has a kinship with one or more of these attitudes. Some men will deny death, while others are so esoteric that death to them is the desired "sleep" so that life "on the other side" can begin. Some men are caught up in an Elijah complex. They think they, like the prophet of old, will somehow miraculously escape death. At the same time, there are men who are forcing themselves to function in the role of a clergyman all the while they are floating about in an empty vacuum. Then there are those ministers who always seem to be smiling and expect others to be incessantly happy along with them. Frequently there are more than a few who are unconsciously caught up in the melodramatic life-style. Whether it is at a birth or a death, a wedding or a tragedy, they always seem to look and talk the same.

While I studied in denominational schools, I saw men who were anxious and uncertain about themselves. I have witnessed across denominational ranks that many ministers are anxious about life and death. In various meetings, from interdenominational ministerial meetings to university conferences, I have felt that many of my colleagues are miserable. They are perhaps trying to use their role, their work, to discover both who they are and how they can deal with the struggles of life and death. In graduate studies and in parish settings I have had men tell how they have many ambivalent feelings about themselves and their work. Recently I have wondered if the fact that some ministers conduct many funerals does not tend to enhance their sense of immunity to death. After all, while people all around them are dying, they keep on living!

I feel beyond question that as ministers we cannot be healthy, effective instruments of God's redemptive love and grace until we have squarely faced and dealt with *our own* feelings. How many men fail in a counseling situation because they cannot get around or work through their own feelings aroused by the context. I have observed on numerous occasions that this problem has stifled the effectiveness of any ministry that might have been offered during the crises surrounding death. Kübler-Ross noted with amazement that the sole communication many ministers offered a dying person was either to read a stated prayer or to read a passage from the Bible. No attempt was made to relate to or to understand the person.[3]

C. Charles Bachmann included in his book, *Ministering to the Grief Sufferer*,[4] a report of a survey of 1,000 New York ministers. The survey dealt with the current parish patterns and practices concerning death. From the data he collected, he was able to pinpoint clinically that ministers have a difficult time being objective about their own deaths. Some men will tend to ignore their own feelings, while offering comfort and assurance to grieving persons.

Others will feel guilty and anxious that they are speaking words they have not internalized for themselves. Certainly those who have deep problems with death are too psychologically crippled to be able to handle grief therapeutically. Not only is there the difficulty of helping others in their grief, but also such a minister lives the uncomfortable life of repressing his own personal grief. The guilt—real or neurotic—that exists in the grieving person may be paralleled by the minister. Every minister is a human being and need not feel guilty about having strong emotions that are stimulated by the separation anxiety over the loss of a significant person or thing.

It does appear that we have witnessed over a half century of increasing emphasis on the developing intelligence of man—an emphasis that dates back several centuries. In this process men traditionally have been taught to work and to think. Men are not supposed to express feelings and emotions—especially they do not cry. Having lived my childhood during this time, I can attest to the numerous occasions I heard little boys being admonished:

> "Now, be a little man and don't cry."
> "Big boys don't cry."
> "Brave men never cry."
> "Don't be a baby and cry."
> "Only little girls cry when they're hurt."

Unquestionably this technique may have suppressed a tearful scene at that moment. But, far more significant, it has helped to implant the idea that men are to relate emotionlessly to life.

If it is possible, the ministerial models have often given the rising minister even more fuel for such an outlook on life. While there is one group of ministers who are the practical jokesters who play the melodrama to the hilt, there is also a large body of solemn, passive "men of the cloth." When I think back on my childhood, I never recall seeing any minister expressing deep emotions. I am not considering laughing at one another's attempts to be humorous as a revelation of feeling, nor am I referring to the loud, shouting monotone used in preaching. I mean I failed to see the disclosure of one's hurt and one's joy on the part of the ministerial models I observed as a youth.

Whatever the wellspring from which a minister draws his models or obtains his background of feelings, ultimately he has to be responsible for what he does and how he deals with his feelings. I feel I cannot overstress at this point the basic, overarching significance of a minister's recognizing and dealing with his own feelings, particularly those that concern his relating to life and death. More than one psychiatrist has written that studies show that a person who has been at death's door once never fears it thereafter. I am not sure what all the dynamics of this statement disclose. But I do sense that, once a person has honestly faced the reality of death firsthand, it is no longer such a fearful experience.

I am not suggesting that every minister should put himself into a position in which he could die so that he could face death fearlessly. However, I do feel the minister has something to learn from this study. That is, if he would ever allow himself to come face to face with the fact he will die, perhaps he could then internalize this fact. And after accepting his own death, a minister is then free to relate to the dying and the bereaved. What he offers then is not mere sympathy, but genuine empathy. And that empathy comes not from a routine professional, but from a compassionate, caring man.

I read of Dr. Claude Thompson, the late minister/professor of systematic theology, Candler School of Theology, Emory University. When in his sixties he learned he had a malignancy. As he meditated about his condition, he said that he expressed four things to God:

(1)  He told God he could die;
(2)  he told God he would be happy to experience divine healing;
(3)  he told God he would be willing to live under a handicap; and,
(4)  he told God there was one thing he was unwilling to do, and that was to endure his illness alone, on his own strength.

As he drew nearer his impending death, Dr. Thompson preached his last sermon. He entitled it, "How Would You Like to Die?" He reflected in that sermon both his acceptance of death and the learning, growing experience he had felt in the recent months.

One of the central truths that came through that sermon was that he had learned to live one day at a time and to commit each day to God. He confessed how often in the past he had been mixed up like Bre'r Rabbit with Tar Baby—fighting with much to-do but getting all stuck! He said the experience of facing death brought his family closer together. Prayer had become more meaningful, and simple things now brought more joy to the family unit. He also stated that facing death reminded him of his debt to others. And finally he declared that he realized the growth of his Christian faith was anchored in the future. As a Christian, old things pass away and all things become new. Thus Dr. Thompson sought to live life as Christ gives it—life that is beyond the reach of death!

## PREPARATION FOR GRIEF

One valuable aftermath of a minister who reckons with his own inevitable death is that he becomes a potentially valuable resource person. Because of his unique role—relating to the whole family and interpreting the truths of God's word—a minister can do a great deal to help prepare his parishioners for death and grief.

Some of the greatest sources of help in trouble come from what one does in advance. The individual who has the faith to withstand the crisis of death does so on the basis of what he has developed before the emotional storm arises. The minister can aid in the process of developing a reservoir of emotional and spiritual strength. He can do this as an individual, and he can enable the church to play an important role in helping a Christian to anticipate and to prepare for death as a part of life. He can lead the church so it can be ready to sustain both the one dying and the bereaved family.

*Preach and teach the meaning of life and death.* Most ministers will deal with the issues of a meaningful life in Christ or with the promise of life to come. However, more men need to treat the basic fact of death head on, certainly not less than once a year. The place most parishioners would hear him is still in the setting of the morning worship on Sunday.

Just as a minister should not shy away from preaching about life and death, neither should he neglect teaching this subject. The youth of today are flocking to high school and college courses that teach about death. The minister is missing a great opportunity to offer a Christian word on the subject if he fails to help his parishioners understand what is going to happen—that death is going to come, and why a person will feel as he does in the grief experience.

One short-term course on death we offered the adults in our church included the use of several professionals. One session was led by a lawyer, one by a physician, one by a funeral-home director, and two by me. Also one night was given to visiting the funeral home. This learning experience provided an opportunity for our people to feel secure about asking some burning questions they had felt for a long time. It also enabled them to learn a great deal about various facets of death from different Christian professionals.

Another way in which a minister can aid is to use his preaching/teaching role to enable persons to clarify their present family relationships. A great deal of the neurotic guilt felt after the death of a family member could be avoided if persons were able to express their negative feelings directly, if they were able to confess their guilt and seek reconciliation, if they were able to recognize immature relationships and try to find a more mature manner of relating, and if they were able to express their feelings—warm, loving feelings—both verbally and nonverbally. It may be interesting to some to note that not all the preparation for grief is limited to talking about death. There is a great deal to do in terms of how we live now that will affect how we are going to grieve later. And this certainly includes the ability to receive and accept the affirmation of oneself as a person of worth and value.

When I preached the first time specifically about life and death I was anxious about how my parishioners would respond. I was both relieved and challenged to see how readily they grasped and discussed what I had said. The sermon talk-back that followed brought out one of the largest groups we ever had and some of the most open, honest, direct questioning we ever experienced. Not long after this sermon, I conducted a worship survey in which sermons were evaluated and requests for future sermons were made. I was impressed to note that a sermon on the Christian view of death ranked near the top of the most meaningful sermons. Also, this theme was at the top of future sermons requested.

*Be willing to talk about and plan for death.* A minister need not feel limited to specific times of preaching or teaching about death. There are numerous other opportunities to talk to Christians concerning death, in both formal and informal settings. I mentioned above a course offered during our church training period. But I have also experienced healthy group discussion during meetings of our retired adults, during Bible study periods, as well as in special study groups.

If a church member knows he can turn to his minister with confidence and assurance, often he will be able to bear his fears and other feelings about death. Indeed, more than a few church members have made funeral arrangements with me in advance of their death. These plans can be a blessing to the family, both in terms of the cost and the emotional strain of trying to determine what kind of funeral arrangements their loved one would desire. I have witnessed the relieved expression of terminally ill persons who have talked with me and made concrete arrangements for their funeral. Some families have gone on to the funeral home to select the casket and vault before death occurred. Often I have responded to the request to accompany the family on this mission. Some people might think this is a morbid task. However, I see no difference in purchasing a grave site and selecting a casket. Almost everyone has done the former prior to death.

*Plan a Christian funeral.* A minister can help the family in advance of death by giving a description of what a Christian funeral is conceived to be. I have openly stated that I prefer to have the funeral of a church member in the church sanctuary. In this place the family can experience worship through the encounter with God in a familiar setting.

Both in actual practice and in what I say on the subject, my parishioners have discovered that I view the funeral not as a morbid, dreary experience nor a time of pious eulogizing. They know that I expect the music, the Scripture, and the brief meditation to be a time of praise and celebration of God's gifts of life and love. When church members perceive their minister's interest in this subject, they will be more ready to do one of two things. Either they will ask his assistance in preplanning the funeral, or the minister will be among the very first persons the family will call when death occurs. Thus the minister is an active factor in the funeral arrangements from the earliest stages. I have requested that I be involved. Members of my church know I am serious and they welcome such an opportunity.

Each of the three above topics dealing with preparation for grief are described in more detail in a separate chapter. Chapter one includes some of the material I have used in preaching and teaching about death and grief. Chapter three is concerned with relationships with the dying and his family. And chapter four gives a rationale for a Christian funeral.

A minister can conduct a number of funerals a year and never be involved emotionally. In order to stand the strain of constantly associating with the bereaved, he may put his emotions in neutral and sustain only a superficial relationship. The other option is the minister who can be comfortable in expressing his humanness, his emotions, his inadequacies, and his awe at the mysteries of life and death.

We cannot deny death. We cannot master death. We should not try to hasten death to avoid the difficulties of this life. Actually, we as ministers, along with all others, can live to the fullest only when we face and accept the reality of our own deaths. While this must be a frightening experience for non-Christians, we as Christians have the assurance that God does not forsake us in death. When a minister develops this attitude toward death, he can impart faith, calm, and hope to worried, anxious, distressed persons.

We can boldly declare that Christ is our Lord now and in the life to come. What comfort to frightened and troubled hearts!

# 3
# Ministering to the Dying and His Family

Out of their own fear to admit that death will come to them and those close to them, many families play games while their loved one dies alone. What a waste to spend the last few days one has on this earth with a loved one while shallow, empty, deceitful conversation is all that is exchanged. Everyone fears death, but the fear of dying can be greater than the general fear of death. And most especially the average person is fearful of dying alone—helpless, dehumanized, institutionalized, forsaken.

I have heard more than one family say they did not want to break the spirit of their loved one by saying that death was imminent. For awhile I was deceived by this approach. But I came to recognize that the dying person usually senses he is dying. Indeed, he often signals his readiness and desire to talk about his death. The problem is not with the spirit of the one dying. The difficulty lies at the feet of those healthy family members who do not have enough confidence or understanding to stand by their dying loved one—honestly, supportively, simply, and courageously.

C. S. Lewis gives eloquent testimony to the meaning of

conversation between the dying person and the family. He wrote of the last night before his wife died: "It is incredible how much happiness, even how much gaiety, we sometimes had together after all hope was gone. How long, how tranquilly, how nourishingly we talked together that last night."[1]

I will never forget the first time I talked specifically about death with a dying person. It happened quite by accident. Early one morning I was summoned to the home of this woman who was terminally ill with cancer. The manner and words of the family caused me to feel they had already told her she was at the point of death.

Since I had come to the point of wanting to deal honestly with my parishioners, I perhaps read my own feelings into the context. At any rate, I went to sit alone at her bedside at dawn, after the woman had spent a painful, sleepless night. Within a few moments I asked her how she felt, knowing that her death was near at hand. In a very positive, even joyful manner, this quiet Christian woman talked incessantly for more than a half hour. She spoke of her past, her children, her husband, and her Lord. She gave witness to her calm assurance of the presence and redemptive power of Christ in her life.

That night the family told me she talked with them about her feelings about death after I left. She then relaxed and slept soundly for several hours without any medication. She died before midnight. It was only when I talked with the family after her death that I realized I was the first person to talk directly and honestly with her. Because of what I saw happen in the life of that woman and her family, I decided that night I should do all I could to enable dying persons and their families to talk about death with each other.

An important task every minister has is to encourage families to sense and to respond to the dying person's readiness to talk about impending death. Even though more people are talking about death in general terms now, it still is difficult to talk with a close loved one who is dying. However, I feel that postfuneral ministry can be strengthened by this predeath ministry. Grief can be much more focused after a person has had the opportunity to talk with a loved one before his death. The dying person will signal willingness to talk about death, though not be interested in or able to do so constantly, any more than a person can look directly into the sun. It is important to be perceptive and ready when the dying person wants to talk.

## THE BURNING DESIRE TO BE UNDERSTOOD

Everyone wants to be understood. Especially do family members want to be understood by one another. The time such compassionate perception is desired is never more crucial or intense than when a person is near death. Unfortunately, instead of the dying person being understood, frequently he has to help the living who surround him to perceive their emotions more clearly.

When I was in seminary, a classmate was suddenly stricken with a rapidly advancing form of leukemia. I had been close to this man since college days. One day, while I visited him in the hospital, several other seminarians crowded into the room to pay their respects. After this had continued for some time, he asked me to request the others to leave. He then broke down and cried about how frustrated he had been. He said people came to see him and literally drained him of his physical and emotional strength. Many of the students he did not know by name. They came offering their pious platitudes about faith, courage, healing, and victory over death. They did not really come to share with my friend or to hear what he felt. He also sensed they came out of guilt becuase they had not known him before. And he knew they came because they were anxious that God would allow a promising young divinity student to die. Instead of helping him, my friend was having to take care of these visitors who were bothered by death. To preserve his energy, I requested the dean of students on behalf of my friend to limit the visitors to his family and closest friends.

In our fractured, partial attempts to live, we seldom talk with others, even those who are the closest to us, about either the deep meaning and purpose in living or the event of death. At the point of his martyrdom, rather than to lie to save his life, Sir Thomas More was pleading with his wife to talk with him about his impending death, to tell him she understood he was going to die. There was a profound sense of relief when she acknowledged she understood and affirmed what he was doing. And it is not just the martyrs who want to be understood. Everyone has the basic desire to have those close to him acknowledge and help interpret not only death, but also the life that precedes it.

## REACTIONS OF THE DYING

We can help both the dying and their families when we help parishioners to understand the basic, normal reactions of dying persons. The classic description of this process was written by Dr. Kübler-Ross in her study of doctors and theological students who worked with terminally ill patients. Her book, *On Death and Dying*, needs to be read with careful thought by all clergy. She lists the following five differing, and most often progressive, reactions among dying patients. The concept of these reactions is not limited to dying persons. They are quite similar to those of persons who face surgery, experience trouble, or lose something or someone close to them—from a pet's death to a divorce. (Chapter 7 gives a detailed section on types of grief.)

*Denial* is the first reaction toward impending death. "No,

not me; it cannot be true." In the midst of the shock of realizing we will die, we usually pretend it is not true, or we ignore what we know to be true. It is probably at this level that most healthy persons function because we believe that death is nowhere near. Rather than face the reality of death, we reject it as a personal possibility, even when we are told that we will soon die.

*Rage and anger* are the second reaction. "Why me?" Why could it not be someone less able, responsible, vivacious, and creative—someone older, or at least someone whose life is useless? The thought of having life disrupted and projects incompleted calls forth all kinds of anger and hostility. It is quite likely that some of the timidity about talking with persons concerning death stems from seeing dying persons in this second stage of their reaction. Thus people decide they should spare the dying patient such an experience. The person who has been well but now is facing death may often direct anger toward God, who created people that die.

*Bargaining* is the next reaction of the person who learns he is near death. "Yes, me, but . . . ?" Often the bargaining takes place with God, and it is an attempt to postpone death a little longer. As though one could gain a prize for good behavior, people promise everything, from dedicating their lives to God to committing their vocations to ministry through the Church, if God will only let them live. While at times there can be some genuine reckoning with God, one never genuinely bargains with him. As I understand him, God simply does not function that way! He cannot be bought! Lives may be dedicated to God at birth or at any point in life, but not as a means to stay the time of death. Seldom is such an attempt sincere anyway. This is a preliminary stage of depression.

*Depression* on a deeper level is the next reaction. This is the time the person begins to get ready to die. He can say, "Yes, me," but he is still flooded with despair and depression. Death is seen as inevitable, but yet the one who will die is not ready to accept his death in the fullest sense. He anticipates the loss he will experience—everyone and everything he has ever loved!

*Acceptance* is the final reaction. "I accept the fact that I am going to die." It is not necessarily a happy stage, but it does include some sense of completion and often inner peace. It is an emotional victory when one can acknowledge his limitations as a human though no one who appreciates life is anxious to leave it.[2]

When dying persons are overwhelmed with feelings of hopelessness, helplessness, and isolation, it is difficult for them to struggle through their experiences alone. A minister can assist the Christian person to join with acceptance the element of hope. While God has allowed evil to be present in this world, he has demonstrated through the Cross and the empty tomb that in his mystery he can bring life, light, and hope. Thus a Christian can hope to live as long and fully on this earth as possible, but still feels the assurance of God's presence beyond this life.

"I never think he is quite ready for another world who is altogether weary of this . . ."[3] is the expression one writer used to describe a healthy emotion in the face of death. While not longing for death to come, we can accept that it will come to each of us. A minister can help both the dying person and his family feel more comfortable, less anxious and guilty when he recognizes that these are normal feelings. A lot of emotions have been choked off in stages two or three because people did not understand these were feelings that must be worked through.

In reviewing the reactions of dying persons, it is important to note that many persons try to deal with their inevitable death with force. That is to say, they might change doctors in an effort to disprove their illness is terminal. They might claim to terminate their belief in a God who would allow this to happen to them. Or they might piously claim that what has happened is God's intended will. Therefore no one can do anything about it. But the implication is that if they could do anything, they would surely deal harshly with God for the way he is treating them.

*Prayer* is an umbrella reaction to the prospect of dying. The minister can be of great help to a person when he is perceptive of the dynamics of prayer. Many terminally ill persons use prayer in their efforts to bargain with or to manipulate God. In fact, some ministers seem to pray for healing with such assurance that God's healing power is unconditional. But when healing does not come, the dying person is depressed. He is left with the feeling that God has rejected him or that his faith is inadequate.

Prayer can be a vital force in the life of a dying person. But there are two elements a minister needs to help that person and his family bear in mind. One is that we believe in spiritual healing as long as it includes death. We should not pray for God to make a person whole and feel the only way that can be done is to give new strength in this life. The ultimate making whole of an ill person who is in Christ is to allow death in this life and to know fellowship in Christ that is complete.

The other element of prayer with the terminally ill is that healing may assume a form other than physical. As I have described earlier, there are more painful ways to die than physical death. The meaningless life or the lonely life is little more than dying daily. One man prayed for healing and he was convinced he was healed. But after a brief remission his illness returned. However, this man lived out his days confident in Christ's love for him. He said: "I prayed for healing, and God healed me. He didn't heal my body, but He healed my mind and my spirit. He healed me of fear, of resentment, of bitterness, of worry for my family. This is God's answer to my prayer."[4]

## Needs of Dying Persons

It may be a bit presumptuous to attempt to speak of the needs of dying persons. Indeed, some of these have already been described, and others that might be mentioned are too vast for one volume. While recognizing these limitations, I feel there are two specific needs a minister can approach with added sensitivity.

*Allow a person to die in life.* This statement has numerous implications. There are two particularly significant ones. The first is that a person deserves to be told that he is living out his final days with a terminal condition. It is both deceitful and unfair to allow a person to die without affording him the opportunity to review and evaluate his life when it is at all possible to do so. Neither does it seem right for a person to be robbed of his final opportunity to express his love and appreciation of his family. In ancient societies the final days and hours were times of blessing and being blessed.

The other significant feature I would mention is that a patient needs to be allowed to die his own death with dignity. And this often would involve not artificially prolonging the process of dying. What I am saying is not to be confused with mercy killing. The latter actually takes a person's life to free him from suffering physically or mentally. Dying with dignity is choosing to allow the decayed, worn-out body to run its natural course without being propped up. Surely every measure possible would be employed when the illness first sets in. And if the patient is ten or twenty instead of eighty, a great deal more time and effort would be spent striving to prolong the person's life. What I am feeling was expressed well by one of my members whom I visited recently in the hospital. As she described her lack of strength due to several strokes, a heart attack in the last year, and now gallstones, she said she well expected declining health. After all, she had lived seventy-eight years, and she did not anticipate living forever. She went on to add that she did not want to live forever in her present body. She knew it was becoming too old!

Shakespeare's Julius Caesar declared: "Cowards die many times before their deaths; the valiant never taste of death but once."[5] I am concerned about a dying person's right to decide how to live his final days. This includes both the omission of medical aids to prolong existence when life is spent and the provision of drugs to alleviate terminal suffering, even if the drugs may hasten death. It does not seem fair to me that a terminally ill person has to weave in and out of death and life many times before he dies. Death can—indeed, should—have dignity.

*Allow a person to be with family and be alone.* This statement seems to be paradoxical. And yet there are two important concepts to be held in tension by the minister who seeks to interpret the dying person's needs to the family. A dying person is usually rushed off to the hospital, where he is kept busy by machines and frequently isolated from family and friends. Recently more and more persons have been feeling that this setting is unsatisfactory for the person who is terminally ill. On the one hand the hospital is committed to the task of helping to heal. The staff often has neither the time nor the interest to minister to the dying. On the other hand, a dying person needs the privilege of spending time with his family during his last days.

The "hospice" is one solution to this problem. England has the first such institution, a place restricted to the terminally ill. Its sole purpose is to help provide a good death. Everyone—including children and pets—is encouraged to visit. Hospices are being organized in the United States—the first one is to be constructed in New Haven, Connecticut. The key to this concept is the provision of adequate medication, compassionate care, professional counseling, and the opportunity to be with one's family.

When communication is honest and open between the dying patient and his family, there will be sufficient understanding so that the family can spend good times together and still allow the person some time to be alone. A very normal part of dying is the act of withdrawal. While a dying person does not desire to be abandoned by his loved ones, he does need some time to complete his preparation to sever his ties with this life.

Surely understanding remains a key need of the dying person. When he feels this from his family, his minister, and significant others, he can be free to express his feelings and make the adjustments he needs to make. The process of preparing to die was expressed well in the letter Dr. Kübler-Ross received from a young dying mother: "We had a wonderful Christmas. It has been almost two years since the diagnosis, and I am thankful I feel as good as I do. Trying to keep up with five boys wears me down real fast. But you get a little less particular about the dust in the corners. My husband and I have gone through so much, but we have lived life fuller and enjoyed it more than some people do in a whole lifetime. Nobody but the Lord knows what is going to happen, so I am going to enjoy life right now."[6]

An honest attempt to provide an adequate ministry to the dying and to his family may open the way for more meaningful living for whatever length of time that may be. And, after all, the basic thrust of the Christian life is focused on quality and not quantity. It is hopeful that both the dying person and his family might deepen the quality of their relationships to each other and to God.

# 4
# The Christian Funeral and Its Purpose

From the approaches I have observed, it would seem that many ministers consider the funeral to be either a cultural tradition or a liturgical accident. That is to say, it seems as though little or no thought is given to any system or order that would lend strength and meaning to the bereaved family. Either some ministers are repeating by rote the style of funeral they experienced in their past, or they are poorly executing an approach they have happened to discover.

While I do not want to overdo my reaction, I am concerned that a minister develop a healthy view of a Christian funeral. I have described my concept of a Christian funeral both in sermons and in writing to my parishioners. I have set the stage for our involvement together in a funeral by publicly declaring that I appreciate the family who calls me at the same time the funeral director is called. This enables me to begin my ministry to them and help plan an appropriate experience of Christian worship. As the representative of Christ and his church, I can convey through my presence the abiding love and strength of God.

I openly state that I prefer to have the funeral of an active church member in the church sanctuary. This is the proper place to recognize the mystery of death. After all, this is where both the gift of life and the gift of Abundant Life were acknowledged. The sanctuary is the place where prayers of petition and thanksgiving have been offered, one's faith has been declared, bonds of love have been sealed, and the birth and dedication of children have been celebrated. Through the memories of high experiences in the sanctuary and the realization of its dedication as the place for corporate worship of God, the use of this room can be a valuable means of facilitating a worship experience for the grieving family.

## THE PURPOSE OF THE FUNERAL

There are numerous healthy purposes for a funeral. As a minister sorts through and internalizes some of these reasons for himself, he is better able to impart this understanding to his parishioners. Then both he and they will approach the funeral hour better able to celebrate it as a Christian event. While the following list is not intended to be all-inclusive, it states some of the significant purposes of a Christian funeral.

*It provides a turning point.* In every important experience of life, we need a focal point, a point of reference. A funeral can help bereaved persons to face and deal with the reality of death. Frequently a well-conducted Christian funeral can be the time of enabling bereaved persons to begin facing the rest of their lives with meaning and courage. While the funeral is not a time to ignore or abandon grief, it can be the kind of affirmative experience that will prevent one from falling into uncontrollable or neurotic grief. Guilt can be relieved and strength be undergirded through a truly Christian funeral.

*It encourages openness to God's love.* Some people have not recovered from a state of shock when they come to the funeral. Others have not gone beyond feelings of hostility and indifference toward God for allowing death to come to a loved one. Therefore the funeral can be a time of encouraging those who grieve to recognize that God loves them. He has always loved them in the past, he loves them now, and he will always love them in the future. He loves them in their grief. Indeed, he will be with them in their grief. Unfortunately the love of God for the bereaved family is too often a missing word in funerals.

*It provides a bridge over the fear of death.* Many of the persons present at a funeral are not thinking as much about the dead person as they are about themselves. The fact that a loved one has died only accents the fact that each person present will also die. A well-thought-out funeral can be an aid in bridging the chasm between the fear of death and the hope for life eternal. This need not be done in a maudlin, sentimental way. But as God's work and presence are affirmed, the fear of being abandoned by God can be arrested. A strong bridge can be established on the basis of God's promise never to forsake us, never to leave us alone.

*It reaffirms belief in the Resurrection.* When God is praised for the triumph of his love over death, belief in the Resurrection can be affirmed in a joyful manner. This experience can draw the mourners closer to God, enable them to feel comforted concerning the person who has died, and give them courage to face the prospect of their own deaths.

*It offers a significant occasion for worship.* Of all the reasons for a funeral, the central one is the opportunity for encountering God in worship. This involves some thought and planning on the part of the minister. A well-designed order of worship that includes great music of the church, appropriate Scripture, and a brief meditation can help transform a distressed person.

## LEADING A CHURCH TOWARD A POSITIVE CHRISTIAN FUNERAL

The above are some of the significant purposes of a

Christian funeral. On the other hand there are some things which are *not* part of a Christian funeral. It is not a time to display either the dead body or the number of flowers accumulated. While flowers do symbolize the Resurrection, they should be kept at a minimum in the sanctuary. Those who want to pay a lasting tribute to the life and witness of a Christian person could do so through contributions to church memorials or to medical research. While I do not initiate this element in the discussion with a bereaved family, I welcome the opportunity to assist a family in finding alternatives when they desire to move away from a cultural, somewhat pagan, show. Special memorial gifts can be more lasting than an extravagant amount spent on flowers, casket, and vault.

The funeral is not a time for a long oration or a wearisome eulogy. I feel a minister should not employ the funeral to misuse the emotions of the family by trying to manipulate any type of response to God. The funeral is not an occasion to parade ministers before the people. Neither is the funeral a setting to flaunt the deceased's accomplishments. The funeral is not a repetition of culture, whatever that may be in a particular setting, and neither is it a display of pagan rituals.

I feel a church can be led toward a positive Christian funeral when a minister avoids the negative pitfalls and seeks to build something creative and positive. Then not only what he says about funerals, but also how his parishioners regard his conducting of funerals, will encourage families to request strong, positive Christian funerals for their loved ones.

For too long the emotions of the bereaved have been misused at funerals. I feel this is not a time to try to wring out all of the wailing and moaning, neither is it an occasion to appear a Spartan martyr. The funeral is a time to provide a foundation for living the rest of life without a loved one. Grief needs to be worked through, but this task cannot be fully accomplished in the funeral alone. In that hour only one person is able to talk about his feelings—the minister!

During the past several years I have worked with families to design an order of worship for the funeral. This approach has gone a long way toward leading people to see the funeral in a more positive light. As I work with the small group in the family, they are able to see my concept of a funeral in a personal way. Then, as the church shares in the corporate worship of the funeral, their level of expectation and appreciation for it is raised. More and more, instead of listening to tear-jerking solos, the people at the funeral are able to join in singing great hymns of the Christian faith.

Both the economy and the meaning of words make a big contribution toward a positive concept of funerals. Job's friends sat silently with him for a week, offering him the support of their presence. But then, when they spoke, they ruined it all by what they said. As ministers we need to spend time with the family and with ourselves before a funeral. As we thoughtfully seek appropriate ways to offer support to bereaved persons, maybe we can be freed of trying to say everything or trying to defend God. And perhaps we can abandon our fear of not being believed. When we are confident in God's love and presence in the hour of death, we will not have to preach lengthy sermons to convince both ourselves and others that God is there.

I remember the first funeral I had in a new parish. It was for a lady I had seen briefly only one time. I did not know what to say for this one who had died quite suddenly. I searched the Scriptures for words of comfort and hope. I went into that funeral still not knowing what I would say. But much to my amazement, when I had read from the Old Testament, prayed, and then read from the New Testament, I felt more calm. I sensed that as I read from Philippians about the meaning of God's overwhelming peace that his presence had engulfed all the worshippers. (Phil. 4:7) I concluded the funeral with the benediction. I did not attempt to preach a sermon or give even a brief interpretative meditation. After the funeral and later by mail both family and friends expressed their appreciation for the simplicity and strength of that funeral.

I seldom conduct a funeral without having a three- to five-minute interpretative meditation. But I have felt confident ever since the funeral I just described that I need not attempt to say a great deal in order to defend God or myself in the face of death. Through careful, thoughtful preparation I can, in a brief funeral, help a family to discover afresh God's presence and love.

## THE USE OF A PALL

Recently more churches are reinstituting the use of a pall. Since this custom has been eliminated by the average church, a word should be included on this subject.

Every funeral has pallbearers, but probably few people know what the pall is. It is a cloth used for many centuries to cover the casket. Usually it is purple or black, and it has a cross or a monogram of Christ on it. According to my understanding, there are two basic reasons for using the pall. One is that it covers the casket with a symbol of Christ. Thus, as a soldier's casket is covered with the flag of his country, the Christian soldier's casket is covered with a symbol depicting the Lord of his life.

A second reason for using the pall is to indicate that before God we are all equal. While this is true in life, this fact becomes eminently apparent in death. Therefore, as the pall covers the casket in the sanctuary and at the gravesite, there is no cause to think about the expensiveness of the casket or the flower sprays. Attention is focused instead on the witness of one whose life has been committed to God in Christ. Position in life or accumulation of wealth bears no influence when a person encounters God face to face.

The pall is more than a means of saving the family money, though this might be the case in many instances. The pall can provide an additional symbol of the dignity of death and the celebration of God's love for us through Jesus Christ. In most funerals when the pall is used, the church furnishes it and the funeral director returns it to the church following the graveside service and burial.

## FORMS OF BURIAL

Over the centuries there have been a number of different forms of burial. Beginning with the earliest times, these include exposure to the elements, animal consumption, embalming to conserve, water, cremation, and earth burial. For the past few centuries we have experienced principally the earth burial. It is interesting to read that the early Christians had no qualms about being burned at the stake or consumed by wild animals. But later in history the Church has backed away from cremation.

However, a more thoughtful consideration of the biblical teaching on the human body does not cause any concern for how the body is disposed of. Our relationship to Christ is not affected if we are lost at sea, consumed in a fiery crash, buried in the ground, or cremated. Just as God was responsible for the creation of this body made of clay, he will be responsible for the form we take when we meet him face to face.

I sometimes have the feeling that people delude themselves with the idea that they somehow preserve the dead when they place them in airtight caskets and bury them in sealed vaults. Certainly such a form of burial slows down the process of the body's return to dust. But that makes not one iota of difference in the fact that the person is dead, nor does it affect his relationship to God.

I am not attempting to make a case for cremation as the only form of burial. I only hope that a minister understands it and is comfortable in viewing it as an alternative form of burial. More people are selecting cremation, due to ecological, legal, aesthetic, financial, and emotional reasons. Also, the needs of every bereaved person are not identical. For some the cremation of the body would help clarify the finality of death by removing the fantasy of "preserving the body." For others the viewing of the body for a day or two is important to help them adjust more gradually to the reality of death.

It is interesting to note that some states have laws that oppose cremation. In many instances the body has to be embalmed, even though it will be cremated within a few hours following death. Also a casket is required during this interim period. Frequently a container for the ashes is necessary, thus preventing a simple disposition of remains, which are hygienically pure. Certainly society has lent assistance in perpetuating the feeling that cremation is not exactly proper.

It is important that we maintain a Christian outlook on the dead body and the burial of that body. The minister needs to help the family to guard against worshipping the body or trying to preserve it indefinitely. We need also to examine whether a large amount of money spent for the burial of bodies and upkeep of cemeteries is ultimately wise and responsible.

However the body is buried, the minister can be open to the possibility that the family might choose to have a private burial with a brief family funeral. Then a public memorial worship could be held later. In the instances where this is done, the ministry has seemed to be very effective. The emotional trauma of burial is behind the family. The body is no longer present. The potential of full attention toward the celebration of the worship of God might be enhanced if this sequence of private burial and public worship were followed, whether or not burial were done by cremation. Surely it is an idea to consider seriously.

Not every funeral need be the same. But what is important is that the minister be thoughtful, perceptive, and sensitive as to how he can enable the family to design and participate in a truly Christian funeral. The more a minister achieves this end, the more ready and appreciative his parishioners will be of the ministry of the Christian funeral.

# 5
# Steps to Take When Death Occurs

Until several months ago I would not have envisioned the format of this chapter. A conversation with a funeral director altered my feelings. One day, as my custom is, I made the last of several prefuneral contacts with the family during the hour prior to the funeral. The funeral director stopped me on the way to my car to tell me how effective he thought this ministry was. He said that earlier that week he had had a funeral in which the hour of the service had arrived and the minister had not seen the family at all. It was not a matter of the minister's having to be called in from out of town. He simply had neglected to offer any ministry to the family!

At this late hour the frustrated, hostile, bereaved family had asked the funeral director if he could help them find another minister. As he began to try to work through this awkward situation, the minister suddenly breezed into the home. The family reluctantly went ahead with the funeral under his leadership. But their upset emotions, heightened by his insensitivity, eliminated any possibility of aid or comfort coming from God through him. This man had not taken their feelings into account. Therefore he could not—he did not—minister to them. When I asked the funeral director if this happened very often, he replied that I would be amazed at how lax some ministers are in relating to a bereaved family.

After thinking about the insights into counseling I have gained from the classroom and my own reading, I realized just how many ministry courses and books have sidestepped this problem. Due to the lack of training or of self-confidence, it is difficult for pastors to preach on death and grief or to develop good counseling procedures before and after a funeral. Although they are ordained ministers, many feel incapable of counseling the bereaved persons. But every minister is expected to conduct funeral services. For this reason it seems highly significant that some careful attention be given to the ministry that is common to all ministers—the dealing with death, with the funeral, and with postfuneral counseling.

## When Learning of Death

From the backdrop of my conversation with the funeral home director, I am offering some procedures which I have found to be helpful. Since the minister is not normally present when death occurs, I have found it helpful to go to the family as soon as possible upon learning of death. This contact can be extremely helpful if it is properly done. On the other hand, it can be quite upsetting to the bereaved family.

The purpose of being with the family is neither to cut off their emotions nor to sermonize. The minister who has firmed up his own healthy attitude about death will not find it necessary to try to manipulate the family away from their grief with pious platitudes about faith, bravery, or how good it is to escape this life. Certainly one of the most significant functions of the minister's presence is the symbolic role of God's presence and help in every situation—even in the hour of death.

Ministers cannot help the bereaved verbally as much as they

can assist by uncritical listening and by waiting patiently as the grief begins to spill out. Obviously the timing of the initial visit and the level of emotion expressed by the grieving person affect how much talking should be done. But I have yet to see the time when there was not a great deal for the bereaved to talk out if I were willing to listen with patience, empathy, and compassion.

If the minister arrives during the initial hours following death, it is not essential—or even best—to try to work out the details of the funeral. The minister might terminate this early encounter by asking if there is anything he can do to help. If the family expresses concern about the arrangements of the funeral, the minister will certainly want to follow through with them. Or he may do either of the following: One, say he will be back at a certain time to work through the funeral plans with them, or, two, tell the family when he will be available to conduct the funeral. On a number of occasions the family has asked me to go with them to the funeral home to help in making their selections. I am always pleased to extend the ministry of my presence in this way. I offer no suggestions though, when asked, I will encourage the selection of a less expensive casket, or burial in clothes already owned by the deceased. Certainly this emotional moment is no time to drain the family financially.

I have found they will often ask me to pray when I offer my help. I am comfortable with their asking, though I do not want to force my priestly role upon them. Sometimes I will ask them what they would like me to pray. Often this request will stimulate further conversation, both at that moment and in the further encounters I have with them. When I pray, I do not deny their practical physical, emotional, and spiritual needs. In other words, I do not try to lift unduly their expectations of God in their crisis. I do attempt to reassure them of the presence and love of God, as well as the concern, love, and prayers of their Christian friends.

## Planning for the Funeral

At the appointed time I return to discuss the funeral plans with the family. Whether these were prearranged before death or outlined during the initial visit, I find it helpful to work through several details. The first decisions include the time and place of the funeral. A previous explanation to the church and a good working relation with the funeral directors will normally assure a minister's having a voice in this decision. It should be set at a time mutually convenient for the minister, funeral director, and family involved.

I have made it clear earlier that the sanctuary is the logical place for the funeral of an active church member. Not just in recognition of the dead person, but in the realization that this is where the family have shared many spiritual experiences with their loved one. Some may argue that it would be difficult to return and worship in the place where the funeral was held. I would counter by declaring that an unfamiliar funeral chapel often provides little help or comfort during the funeral. Furthermore, when they did return to worship in the sanctuary, they could be reminded once again of the abiding presence of the God whom they worship. I have observed that the family that plans the funeral in the sanctuary is normally more readily able to identify and work through its feelings about God's role in death. There is not an artificial separation between death and the presence of familiar religious symbols.

I feel it is important to ask the family's counsel on how to order the worship for, indeed, a Christian funeral is a worship experience. I usually begin by asking if they would like the congregation to sing. This leads the family to see that the funeral can be a time of encounter with God in the presence and support of fellow Christian worshippers. When there is congregational participation in the funeral, there is always a printed order of worship. When asked, I stand ready to suggest some of the great hymns of the faith, some of which are included in the final chapter of this book. Seldom do I feel compelled to try to lead a family away from a favorite song, but I do encourage music that is theologically sound and will enrich their faith rather than merely bathe their emotions. Organ music is preferable to theologically weak, sentimental songs. Sometimes I use this suggestion as a means of avoiding a poor choice of music. If the church has trained musicians available at the time of the funeral, then meaningful anthems can be sung.

I ask if there is any particular Scripture reading the family would find helpful. Many leave the selection to me, but more than a few make specific suggestions. Each family seems to appreciate being involved in this part of the planning.

The ministry to the family is further extended by visiting with the larger family, either in the funeral home or the family home. This is not a time for planning. It is a time for the ministry of presence. At the same time, I have been surprised at the number of therapeutic conferences I have engaged in while standing in the corner of a crowded room.

## PROCEDURES FOR A FUNERAL

Under this subject I am including a number of things that may appear mundane, yet are crucial to a meaningful funeral. At the outset I suggest establishing a good working relationship with the local funeral directors. Whatever one's past experiences, it is essential to understand local tradition and to be understood by the funeral director. I realized the importance of this practice when I moved from one state to another. I learned in one place that the minister is expected to lead the procession from the sanctuary. At my first funeral in a new state I started down the aisle and was almost run over by the pallbearers! In that place, the minister was expected to follow the pallbearers and precede the casket. Since that time, some of the first persons I attempt to meet in a new parish are the funeral directors.

A good working relationship with your professional counterpart will assure greater cooperation in scheduling funerals. The best funeral directors will never set the time without first checking with the minister. One good director friend knew I was normally off on Fridays. When an inactive family came to him to make the funeral arrangements without consulting me, there was a question of whether to have it on Thursday afternoon or Friday morning. The funeral director took the liberty of telling the family that he felt Thursday afternoon would suit me better. The family agreed to that time, and when I was asked to participate in the funeral the time had already been set at my convenience.

Another procedural matter is the type of burial. In recent years more people have preferred cremation to the traditional burial. Thoughtful, objective counsel should be given a family on this matter. On the one hand, we as Christians know that cremation is not to be feared. There is nothing in the Christian faith that even requires that we be buried.

The minister who is not acquainted with the procedures of cremation should visit a crematory and a columbarium (the place where the urns repose). While a minister should not attempt to make wholesale support for or a resistance to cremation, he should be aware of the need the family has to see the body after death. This opportunity helps affirm the finality of death. On the other hand, a family should not be pressured to put their loved one on display for the whole community to observe. And I say observe, for I have seen a funeral home that has drive-in windows for public observation of the open casket!

Whatever type of burial is used, many families choose to view the body and to have a family funeral and burial. Then the larger community has the opportunity to join the family in a memorial service. With the burial behind them, the family may be better able to worship God and be comforted by friends. However, we must realize that some people may not be able to endure the funeral emotionally without friends standing by. Regardless of the type of burial, it seems best that the family not view the body in the sanctuary or at the graveside. They will have a private time for this purpose in the funeral home prior to the funeral. The potential strength of ministry during a Christian funeral is disrupted if the family is alternating between acknowledging the spiritual while worshipping God and seeing the dead physical remains before them.

I shall never forget the first funeral in which I assisted. It was an open country church in the foothills. Throughout the long sermon the casket was open right in front of the family. Several times one of the sons—one who had been the black sheep and never become a professing Christian—stood up and wailed as he saw his aged father, while the preacher continued to preach loudly. At one point the son fainted and had to be revived by the funeral director.

After the funeral was concluded in the church, everyone paraded by the open casket, led by the family. The weeping and wailing were almost beyond my comprehension. Thinking the worst was over, I was overwhelmed when, after the graveside rites were concluded, the casket was opened again. I know how emotionally wrung out I was when I left the cemetery. I cannot imagine how the family received any spiritual strength that day.

One final procedural matter is the fraternal order or military burial. When the family requests it, arrangements usually can be made through the funeral director to comply with the family's wishes. Care should be taken to insure the understanding of and cooperation with the military or fraternal group in the planning of a Christian funeral.

## RELATING TO THE FAMILY ON THE DAY OF THE FUNERAL

I have found it extremely helpful to make two visits on the day of the funeral, the first to the home of the family during the hour preceding the funeral. My specific purpose here is to reassure them both of God's presence and support and also of the loving support of their Christian family. Often I do more listening than talking. The overall effect is that of bringing a sense of calm to the family through this ministry of presence.

I leave just prior to the family so I can be in my place to meet them and lead them into the sanctuary. Before I depart I have the immediate family gather in a private room for prayer. In this brief prayer I express my hope that God's presence and the support of Christian friends will be recognized and accepted. Also, somewhat accidentally, I observed that I usually made some positive reference to the weather, since this is frequently a concern of the family. While it is obvious that a bright, warm day is a gift of God, I do not allow the family to forget how the earth needs the rest of cold winter and the refreshing of rain and snow. For as God brings new life to the plants through his seasons, so he gives new life to all who are in him.

After the graveside rites are concluded, I turn to the family. If there are no immediate relatives, I usually greet those seated. When there is an immediate family member, I ask that one if I might walk alongside back to the family car. I then take an arm and walk with and listen to that person.

The second visit is made immediately following the burial. I leave before the family car so that I can await their arrival at their home. I then walk with the same person into the house. I feel that reentry into the house is one of the most difficult experiences for the bereaved loved one. For many, this is the first time the realization of death and the sense of loneliness begin to sink in. I usually take time to sit down with that loved one. This position gives some physical relief to the weary mourner who still has well-wishers streaming by. It also allows some opportunity for me to listen to more memories and feelings that need an outlet. Indeed, I am assisting in the vital mourning process. I make no apology for taking this seat of importance. I remain until I can feel good about the attitude of this particular family member.

My present parish has a helpful tradition. On the day of the funeral several of the ladies provide a meal for the family. Unless the family has another preference, the meal is served at the church. This allows the family a private time apart from the rush and confusion of all those who come and go at home. It is also a tangible expression of the love and interest of the church family.

## FOLLOW-UP MINISTRY

Because of the complexity of grief, a follow-up ministry is a crucial aspect of the process. So vital is this work that I have devoted a later chapter to grief counseling.

As I facilitate positive grief, I make several copies of what was said during the funeral. By giving these to the family, I enable them to renew the sense of strength they found earlier in hearing God's Word. Often they will share a copy with family members or with friends who were unable to attend the funeral.

Everyone wants and needs someone to listen to him and understand. A minister faithfully represents the good news of God in Christ when he offers the strength both of himself and of his church to those who grieve. An effective ministry can be a determining factor in the future lives of grieving adults and children alike. Without question, this conclusion to the steps a minister takes when death occurs is a vital form of ministry through postfuneral grief counseling.

# 6
# A Minister Deals with Death:
# An Example

Using the suggested steps of the previous chapter as a back-drop, this chapter presents a fictitious case history of a funeral. Through this example the reader may look through the lens I use in viewing the process of death, the funeral, and grief counseling. This is the account of Mr. Samuel S. Smith.

## WHEN LEARNING OF DEATH

Mrs. Smith's sister-in-law called early Saturday morning to tell me the police had just come to tell Mrs. Smith her husband had been killed in an automobile accident. Evidently the car that hit him was being driven by a man who had been drinking throughout the previous night. He had run head-on into Mr. Smith's car while Mr. Smith was on his way to work.

The Smiths had not been active in our church during the five years I had served that parish. As a matter of fact, I had only seen them on two or three occasions. While I was driving across town to their home, I realized this would be an opportunity for the ministry of our church to be felt in the life of this inactive family.

The police were still at the house when I arrived. Mrs. Smith was sitting in the kitchen, trembling and weeping from the shock of the news she had received. I went over and sat down beside her. When I spoke to her, I told her how sorry I was to hear of this tragedy. She thanked me for coming so soon, and then her voice broke as she sobbed while asking why did this have to happen to them. She said she and her husband were so happy. They did everything together. Since her two children were married and gone, he was all she had.

I replied to her that we cannot always find easy answers to the problems and tragedies of life. I said I knew that God does allow all of us to live in freedom on the earth he has given us. The way some misuse that freedom causes others to be hurt, even to die. She passively said she guessed she would just have to accept this as God's will. After all, there is nothing we can do about it when our time comes.

I gently countered this view by saying that God wants the very best for us all the days of our lives. Certainly he is able to know when and how we die, though I do not feel he arbitrarily causes our death at a certain time. I told her there are two things I am sure about. One is that God is acquainted with grief. His only Son was put to death by the hatred of men. And the other thing is that God has promised never to forsake us, in life or death. I told her my hope was that she could claim God's promise to be with her even in that hour. In spite of the tragic death, God had not forsaken her. Mrs. Smith said she was glad I reminded her that God was with her.

At this point the funeral director arrived. Mrs. Smith spent the next half hour or more with the family members coming in and with answering the questions asked by the police and the funeral director. I remained during this time, talking with various members of the family who came to the Smith home. I was also present to determine, with the family and the funeral director, a convenient hour for the funeral.

After the police and funeral director had left, other friends and family members began to arrive. I then went to Mrs. Smith and told her that I would be back later to discuss the funeral with her. I asked if there was anything I could do. She indicated there was nothing, other than to pray for her. I asked her what she would like me to pray. She hesitated a bit, and then said to pray that God would get her through the funeral. We were in the den with two other close relatives and I told her I would pray with her then if she would like me to. She readily said she wanted me to pray. The following is what I prayed:

O God, we thank thee for life and the joy of living and sharing it with family and friends. We thank thee for every good gift that comes from thy hand, especially abundant life through Christ Jesus, thy Son, our Lord. We thank thee that we can open ourselves to thee in joy and happiness as well as in sadness and sorrow.

Father, we confess that we cannot understand all of the mysteries of life and death. We recognize the shock and pain this wife is feeling at her husband's death. While we would long to have some clear word from thee, help us to hear what thou hast said—that thou would never leave us alone. Help us to claim that promise now.

Give to this friend an extra sense of thy presence, love, and comfort. Help her to know that even in a tragedy such as she has experienced that thou will stand by her. Indeed, as she seeks thy leadership, help her to find renewed strength for these dark days. Undergird her through the presence and love of family and friends. Assure her that what she fears she cannot do alone, she can do through thee with the help of others.

Be with her children as they travel to be with her. Watch over her that she may have the ability to live each day at a time. This we pray in the name of Jesus Christ our Lord. Amen.

Mrs. Smith thanked me for the prayer, saying that she felt a calm and a sense of God's presence that she had not known in a long time. She thanked me for coming and for being with her. I assured her of my continued prayerful concern for her and told her I would see her later on that afternoon. Meanwhile, I insisted she should not hesitate to call me if I could be of any assistance. I then departed.

## PLANNING FOR THE FUNERAL

Since I knew the funeral was going to be held on Monday morning, I decided to return to the home later Saturday afternoon to discuss the plans with Mrs. Smith. Just before I came her daughter arrived home. The son in the army would not get home until late Saturday afternoon. It was obvious that Mrs. Smith and her daughter had been sobbing together over their grief.

When Mrs. Smith saw me she managed to smile and introduce me to her daughter, telling her how much I had meant to her because I came just after Mr. Smith died. It did not take me long to realize how close father and daughter had been. Nearly a half hour was spent listening to the mother and daughter express their love and appreciation for husband and father. The disbelief and hurt were deep, and yet they were able to ventilate their feelings in my presence. In the course of their talking about Mr. Smith I learned that he loved to work in the yard and had developed quite a flower garden.

Later on, when I asked, they said they had not given much thought to the funeral plans. They indicated that no specific arrangements had been planned by Mr. Smith. Mrs. Smith had decided that morning to have the funeral service held in the funeral chapel. Since Mr. Smith had been inactive in the church for nearly fifteen years, I did not have strong feelings about the service not being held in the sanctuary.

I began working through the specific aspects of the funeral

by asking what music they wanted. Mrs. Smith said she had seen the congregation sing at a funeral in our sanctuary several months before. Her daughter said she had never heard of it. The two talked about the music and realized they had no definite feelings about what music was used. They did not want a solo, and they knew they did not want any "weepy funeral music." When they had boiled it down, they decided they wanted organ music and were not sure about congregational singing. They asked me what I thought, and I told them I had observed that other families had found it helpful to hear the congregation's participation in a great hymn of the Christian faith. They then decided they would like the service to be worshipful instead of mournful. In discussing this attitude of worship, they decided to change the place of the funeral to our sanctuary, where they felt it would be more appropriate, especially since they wanted to have the congregation sing. The following order of worship is what was worked out. It was printed and distributed to those who attended the funeral.

## THE WORSHIP OF GOD
At the Funeral of Mr. Samuel S. Smith
March 20, 1970

Sacred Organ Music (culminating with "A Mighty Fortress")
Opening Sentence
Hymn No. 286 "O God Our Help in Ages Past"
Invocation
Old Testament Lesson
Prayer
Organ Meditation "Beneath the Cross of Jesus"
New Testament Lesson
Meditation
Benediction
Organ Postlude "Guide Me, O Thou Great Jehovah"
Graveside at Woodlawn Cemetery

The sacred organ music at the beginning included a number of hymns, culminating with the playing of "A Mighty Fortress Is Our God" as the family entered. They left the selection of appropriate Scripture up to me. They stated they did not want a lengthy funeral, and they especially desired a brief graveside service. I told them I agreed with their desire for brevity.

Because Mr. Smith liked them so much, they were allowing flowers to be sent. Anyone who wanted to make a memorial gift was requested to make it to the church's Building Fund. They told me the burial would be in the nearby Woodlawn Cemetery. I was to be in sole charge of the funeral.

After we had completed these arrangements, I asked if there was anything else I could do. They told me there was not, and thanked me for coming and talking with them. I told them I would stop by the funeral home the next evening, at which time I would be able to meet Mr. Smith's son.

I was amazed to learn how many family members Mr. Smith had in our church membership. I knew there were several brothers, but I had not fully envisioned the extended family. My time and interest during the visit to the funeral home on Sunday evening undergirded the ministry I had already begun with the Smith family.

I had the opportunity to meet the Smith's son, who was a career man in the U.S. Air Force. Standing in the corner of the family room, this man bared quite a variety of feelings—from appreciation for his father to his estrangement from his father, both before and after he entered the Air Force. My approach with him was to assure him that God would forgive any wrong he had done against his father. And at the same time God would enable him to draw from the strengths of the experiences and memories of his father to make his life more meaningful. I also encouraged him to talk out with his base chaplain the feelings that would surface in the weeks to come. I tried to help him see he need not feel guilty about having ambivalent or even negative feelings about his father. What was important was for him to express and understand those feelings. He expressed his appreciation for my listening to him and for giving him some assistance with handling his feelings.

## Relating to the Family on the Day of the Funeral

It was a cold, rainy day when I arrived at the Smith home, forty-five minutes before the funeral. The first portion of my visit was spent greeting members of the family and meeting others I had not seen before. Then I asked that Mrs. Smith and her children and their families come apart from the rest of those gathered in the home. When we got into the den with the doors closed, I asked them how they were feeling. They verbalized their anxiety and their continued numbness from the shock they had experienced. I told them that my purpose in being there was to remind them of two things. One was that God loved them and that through his Spirit he would stand by them in the hours to come. The other thing I wanted them to remember was the love, concern, and prayers of their Christian friends. I said that many of those friends would evidence their interest through their presence in the funeral. Others who could not attend would be thinking of them. Then I led them in this prayer:

> Father, we thank thee for being with us when we feel so frightened and alone. Just as the earth needs the winter to rest and the rain to bring forth new growth, remind us that through thy grace and strength, new life can surface in us in the midst of grief and stress. Give each member of this family an added sense of thy presence.
>
> We thank thee for giving us family and friends to express love and strength to us when we are sad and weary. May we search for ways to understand and undergird one another in the hours and days ahead.

Help us that our encounter with thee in corporate worship may inspire new hope and assurance, both in this day and in every day that is given us.

Thank thee, O God, for caring about us at all times. We claim thy promise to be with us now. Give us comfort and courage as we live these hours in the name and spirit of thy strong Son, even Jesus Christ our Lord.     Amen.

Following the prayer I told the immediate family that I would be leaving to be in my place in the sanctuary. They expressed their appreciation for my coming. I said I would see them again after the funeral.

I met the family at the door and led them into the sanctuary. The order of worship was distributed to the worshippers as they entered the sanctuary. (A copy of all the components of the funeral is included in the appendix.)

After the graveside rites were concluded, I turned to Mrs. Smith and asked if I could walk back to the car with her. She talked briefly about how she had managed better than she had anticipated. I also spoke to her son and daughter as they entered the car. Then I got into my car and departed for the Smith's home.

I was at the home when the family car arrived. I escorted Mrs. Smith back into the house. She seemed visibly to give a sigh of relief that the pressure of the funeral was behind her. Again she stated her amazement that she had endured the time with composure. She said that she had felt uplifted by everything I had said and done.

At my request we sat down together. While family members were coming and going about the home, we talked quietly. She expressed her disbelief that her husband had been killed. It all seemed so senseless. She had more to say than at any previous time as to how much she would miss her husband. They had always done so much together and were so devoted to one another. I encouraged her to enrich her life with the memories of the experiences of the good life they had shared together. I also asked her to envision how Mr. Smith would want her to go on living with meaning and purpose. She said she still felt hurt and confused, but that she did not blame God for what happened.

She talked about her son and daughter. She said her husband loved her son more than the son realized. She had been grateful for the attitude he had had about his father since he had come home. She wished her daughter and her family could move back closer to home. She had been quite far away for several years, though they had been trying to locate closer to her home for quite a while.

After listening attentively to her for nearly a half hour, I felt a sense of calm about her. I then got up and made an opportunity to talk with both the son and the daughter. Each of them expressed appreciation for what had taken place that day, as well as the strength they had found in our earlier conversations. I assured all three of these family members of God's love and our church's love for them. I told them I would come again in a few days. After greeting other family members present, I departed.

## FOLLOW-UP MINISTRY

I returned on Thursday, taking with me a copy of Edgar N. Jackson's book, *You and Your Grief*,[1] and several copies of the funeral service, which appears in the appendix. Just Mrs. Smith and her daughter were there. The son had returned to his base. The two ladies were pleased to have an opportunity to talk. They were distressed about the lack of privacy they had experienced for the past several days. Family members and friends alike were coming early and staying late. I explained to them how people will often work off their guilt feelings about their relationships with a deceased person by overreacting when he dies. I encouraged them to go out for a meal and get away from the noise and confusion in the house. I also told them to be comfortable in telling the family members they could feel free to stay, but that she (Mrs. Smith) was going to get some rest. She stated she was exhausted from having had to sit up past midnight every night.

I gave them Jackson's book with this inscription:

Smith Family:

May this book be both an aid in interpreting your grief and a reminder of your church's continued interest to you.

Your Minister,
Robert W. Bailey

First Baptist Church
March 23, 1970

I asked them to read it within the next few days. The length would only require a couple of hours at the most. I indicated that this book would help give some insight into the problems they were already encountering. I also gave them the sobering word that soon Mrs. Smith could expect visitors to be very infrequent.

When I gave them the several copies of the funeral service I had had mimeographed, they thanked me again for what the funeral had meant to them. They were pleased to have the copies, because several family members had asked for them. I told them we would have more in the church office if they needed them.

As Mrs. Smith expressed her appreciation for me and for the support of the church, she said she planned to become active in the fellowship of the church once again. I told her she need feel no obligation to repay us. At the same time I encouraged her to be open to the strength she could find by being with and offering her help to others. It would be important and healthy for her to continue to be able to receive from and give to others. She said she planned to resume her work after a two-week leave.

Both mother and daughter expressed a continued state of numbness from the whole experience. The death seemed so unreal and unnecessary. They both said they had cried several times. I supported their reaction as a normal, healthy one. I said that even knowing of God's love and care does not prevent the loss of a loved one to hurt us deeply.

At this point Mrs. Smith opened up a feeling she had repressed previously. She said she had been feeling guilty. As I explored her feelings with her, I learned that she had some deep-seated feelings that God was punishing her husband and her for not being more committed to him. I reassured her that God does not manipulate our love through such measures. And I stated once again that she should not attend activities at our church with the motive of winning God's pleasure. She does not have to buy God's love—it is hers already.

At the same time I told her that God could help her achieve a positive, redemptive conclusion to this tragedy. I urged her to be receptive to God's many good gifts daily as well as in corporate worship. I also encouraged her not to attend worship solely to relieve her guilt. I sensed that she seemed somewhat embarrassed for having displayed her feelings, so I assured her that she need feel no guilt for what she said or how she felt. On the contrary, God and I were glad she was able to express what was within her. I only hoped that she could face God each day with a more positive outlook because of our conversation. Mrs. Smith was visibly and verbally appreciative and relieved at this explanation.

Sensing her calm, I told them I would continue to think of them and pray for them in the days ahead. I stated that I would be back within a couple of weeks to talk about what they had read. I urged them to contact me if I could be of any assistance to them meanwhile.

Mrs. Smith told me how much my prayers had meant and asked me if I would pray right then for God's strength and courage for them. I prayed:

> Father, we admit we have neither the strength nor the insight to live life apart from thee. Thou art aware of the intense hurt this family has endured. Help them to feel the depth of thy love and the concern of their Christian friends. May we make real and meaningful thy compassion for them.
>
> Give them the courage and strength, the hope and joy that will enable them to face and live one day at a time, knowing that each of us receives the gift of life in such a brief, yet potentially meaningful, span of time.
>
> May thy rich grace and peace that is sufficient for every experience of life enrich and sustain these friends. We pray in Jesus' name.      Amen.

I talked briefly after the prayer and soon left, feeling that both of them were beginning a healthy adjustment to their grief.

I returned to the Smith home in about two and a half weeks. Mrs. Smith had just come home from work. She said things had been going much better since she last saw me. She and her daughter read the book the day I brought it and found it gave both insight and encouragement.

They had gotten away from the house on some of the days

following my previous visit. They also had been able to go to sleep with family members still visiting in the home. Since she had returned to work after a two-week leave, she had discovered her visitors had all but ceased coming. Several evenings she had been completely alone. She felt this was not all bad, however. She had been able to think quietly about some of the feelings she had about her husband's death. She assured me that since our earlier conversation she had not had guilt feelings about what she felt or said, and neither had she felt God was being unjust or was punishing her.

Mrs. Smith and her daughter had returned to worship the preceding Sunday. Mrs. Smith talked about how much that time meant to her. Again she expressed her gratitude for the way in which the worship had been designed and conducted during her husband's funeral. She said she knew he would have been pleased at the simplicity and beauty of the funeral. The family members were grateful along with her for the opportunity of reading the things that had been said at the funeral. She said she was going to follow through on her intent to reactivate her fellowship in our church.

She talked about how she knew Mr. Smith would want her to continue her work and her life with all the meaning she could find. She said she knew it would never be the same without him, but that somehow she would go on. She was pleased to tell me that her son-in-law and daughter had gotten jobs in a nearby community and would be moving back to the area the next month. She said she would feel more secure knowing she could see and talk to her daughter more often.

I terminated this visit by telling Mrs. Smith that I would look forward to seeing her in worship and in other phases of our church life. I encouraged her to enter our Grief Growth Group at its meeting the next month. I assured her of my continued interest in her and asked her to call on me at any time she needed me or simply wanted to talk. She said she would feel free to do so. She asked me to pray with her before I left. I prayed:

> O God, we never know how we can face the difficulties of life until we do so in thy strength and leadership. We thank thee for the courage thou hast given this friend. We thank thee for her attitude and determination. We thank thee for the stronger relationship that is developing between her and thee.
>
> Now we pray that she will continue to sense thy loving presence tomorrow and all the tomorrows thou dost give to her. Remind her that she does not ever go from thy abiding care. Enable us, the Church of Jesus Christ, to provide the environment that will uplift her and call forth the very best from her. This we pray in Jesus' name. Amen.

I assigned a deacon with the responsibility of doing follow-up ministry with Mrs. Smith and her daughter, who had moved to our city. I talked with her on two other occasions. Periodically during the course of the year I checked to get reports from the deacon on how the Smith family was doing.

On Sunday, March 18, a year from Mr. Smith's death, I went to see Mrs. Smith. She was quite happy to have me come. She told how difficult the experiences of the year had been in terms of the adjustments she had to make. She also expressed her surprise that she had found the resources to reorient her life without her husband.

She expressed appreciation for the inspiration of worship in our church. She said she felt that the weekly experiences she had there, along with the visits from her daughter, had largely contributed to her emotional stability. She also was grateful for the visits made by the deacon and his wife. She had continued to find satisfaction from her work, and she anticipated keeping her job until she reached retirement age.

I asked her if there were any problems or concerns that I might help her work through. She said she thought not. She missed her husband still, but had no regrets for the life they had lived and she felt no sense of guilt anymore. She again thanked me for my ministry during the past year, and she stated that she looked forward to the stimulation of weekly worship. She told me that God had surely been with her and she wanted me to continue to pray for her. She asked that I pray then for her to have the courage and strength to live one day at a time. I prayed:

O God, we give thee our humble thanksgiving for being with us in every phase of our pilgrimage of life. We thank thee for never forsaking us, even when we feel we cannot endure what lies before us.

We thank thee for the strength given this friend. We thank thee for enabling her to have the courage and determination to reorient her life after her husband's death. Help her to sense all the meaning and purpose of her life. Draw forth her best gifts so that as she is blessed by thee she can be a blessing to others.

Continue to remind her of our prayers and concerns. Assure her of thy presence and love. Give her the courage and the energy to face and live one day at a time. In the name and spirit of Christ who so lived with thee we pray.     Amen.

After my prayer we talked briefly and I left.

# 7
# Concepts for Grief Counseling

In the survey done by Bachmann, he reported that most of those thousand ministers failed to do postfuneral counseling, either long-term or short-term. An even larger number failed to preach about death and grief. Thus, therapeutic resources appear to be lacking both before and after death. One mental hospital chaplain said the majority of people he deals with are there due to an unresolved grief reaction.[1]

Up to this point the thrust of this book has dealt with death and the funeral. But this is not the end of the story. After the funeral is the time when the real agony begins for the bereaved. Grief becomes more real in the days and weeks following the funeral than it was during the time of shock prior to the funeral.

Grief is complex. It might be understood as the emotional events that take place within a bereaved person. Dynamic psychology taught us that growth comes not by avoiding or escaping grief, but comes best by handling grief constructively. Modern society has made it difficult for the bereaved to deal with their grief. As I will note later in this chapter, most of the reactions in grief are negative ones. But our common tendency is to force people to go from the event of loss to positive reactions of grief. We do this without allowing them to express negative reactions outwardly. We imply that good Christians do not have negative, outward responses to grief.

Grief is normal and inevitable. The minister can aid his parishioners by emphasizing that one need not feel any guilt or lack of faith because one acknowledges the pain of grief. We can help our members not to rush, ignore, or delay their grief. All of us need to work through grief. We are comforted as we mourn, and we are comforted only after we mourn. Indeed, unless mourning is done, growth and reintegration into life cannot take place.

The hazard of not working grief out is that the whole process can bog down, last indefinitely, or ultimately overcome a person. When emotions are turned inward they are apt to surface in some other form. Often it is in a harmful form, such as ulcers, high blood pressure, heart attacks, nervousness, or emotional disorders. Paul Tournier, the outstanding Swiss Christian, wrote that he discovered his full freedom to live after he was released from the pent-up emotions, anxieties, and repressed grief he experienced over the death of his parents.[2] It was because I felt that Tournier's experience of repressed grief is representative of the human family that I wrote this chapter.

## TYPES OF GRIEF

In anticipation of some concepts for grief counseling, I feel it is helpful to consider some different types of grief. Grief is not limited to or triggered solely by death. An awareness of this fact can enable a minister to be more perceptive to the numerous dimensions of grief counseling.

Grief is often felt when there is a break with a significant past, when a person moves or changes jobs—particularly if it is a forced change. Parents feel grief when a child enters school, when he or she leaves home for college or military service, or marries. There is an added sense of grief when the last child departs from home, leaving an empty nest.

There is grief when a favorite object is broken or destroyed, when a pet dies, or when financial loss is experienced. Grief is also felt when a limb is lost, disease is contracted, major surgery is faced, or health fails.

People feel grief when a child runs away from home, a divorce is finalized, or a family member is institutionalized. Grief is also experienced over the loss of youth and over retirement. The latter is especially painful when it is compulsory.

## STAGES OF GRIEF

There are some noted similarities between the stages of grief and the reactions of dying persons. These include the fact that no two people move through grief in the same order of progression or at the same rate. Obviously one significant difference is that after grief is accepted and hope takes root, a living person moves on to establish new relationships, while this is the point of death for the dying.

Many books have been written to describe grief. In addition to Edgar N. Jackson's *You and Your Grief* and C. S. Lewis's *A Grief Observed,* noted earlier, there is Granger E. Westberg's brief book, *Good Grief.*[3] Also, David Bogard recently wrote of a personal experience in *Valleys and Vistas.*[4] My intent here is not to fathom all of the facets in the progressive nature of grief. But it is important for a minister to be acquainted with what might be termed the normal experiences a grieving person endures. It is especially significant for the minister to understand and encourage the negative aspects of grief. Only when these experiences are expressed can a person affirm positive reactions.

*Shock and numbness.* The initial stage is one of disbelief. It is quite natural, and therefore should be acceptable, for a person to shield himself in this manner. During this time a person is emotionless, unable to cry. C. S. Lewis described his sense of numbness in writing: "No one ever told me that grief felt so much like fear. I am not afraid, but the sensation is like being afraid. The same fluttering in the stomach, the same restlessness, the yawning. I keep on swallowing."[5] The reaction to the staggering blow of the death of a loved one is not normally a permanent state. Near the peak of this stage and moving into the next stage, there is a struggle to distinguish between fantasy and reality.

*Emotion is expressed.* Although unable to give way to any emotion initially, emotions later pour out. It is important to reach this point, otherwise one may experience emotional damage. Of course, this stage is difficult for a person who was taught, when growing up, not to cry. While we tend to hide both emotion and grief in our society, in ancient communities people aided each other in working out the grief process. Not only did the ancient Hebrew tear his clothing, put ashes in his hair, wear special clothing, and wail the agony he felt, he also paid mourners to help the grieving family. Friends and neighbors joined in engaging in a long period of mourning.

*Symptoms of distress.* There are numerous descriptive terms that might be employed to depict what mourning people experience. There are several key concepts that portray distress.

**1. Depression.** For a time grieving persons may turn inward and feel very lonely and depressed. To many the reality that death has claimed their loved one, who will never return, is all but overwhelming. Like the clouds that temporarily block the sun from view, depression will normally pass away. Time will help to heal this wound of grief.

**2. Physical reactions.** Because every part of our bodies is tied into one whole being, emotional distress may often surface in a physical symptom. Out of anxiety, we may feel knotted up and unable to function physically. Or, if the recent death was due to an illness, we may feel that we, too, are dying of that disease. If we remain in this stage too long, we can become neurotic over our physical problems.

**3. Guilt.** This is a powerful force for many to deal with. We may feel our loved one died due to our failure to be with him at the time or because of our lack of assistance. Another type of guilt is the feeling that we had been indifferent to the person before he died, or we had failed to express appreciation of or encouragement to the one who is now dead. Guilt can be both neurotic and normal. The first is felt beyond proportion to what we should feel, whereas normal guilt is real. Either way, if it is unresolved, guilt can create more physical symptoms and block reentry into life.

**4. Hostility.** This feeling might be expressed toward anyone who seemed to have a part in the death—from the doctor who failed to save the loved one, or the person who contributed to an accident, to God, who seemed either indifferent or impotent to save this life. It can be helpful for us to vent our hostile resentment, so long as we do not prolong it to the point of becoming married to it!

**5. Inability to function normally.** Due to the varying degrees of distress we feel in our grief, we may be unable to function on our jobs or in our families as we normally would. We simply are too burdened to work everything out in the usual fashion. Perhaps part of the added pressure on contemporary people is due to our unwillingness to grieve more openly. Today a person seldom stays off the job for more than a few days. We tend not to talk about our grief or to give any public display of it. The implication is that we are to return to business as usual. And the busier we are, the better off we are supposed to be. Franklin D. Roosevelt was probably one of the last public persons who grieved openly. In the long-standing tradition, which has now disappeared, he wore a black armband when his mother died. It is difficult for grieving persons when others do not understand or assist them.

*Gradually hope is affirmed.* We need not expect people to quickly regain their vitality for life. At the same time, when they have been given the time to work through their grief, both for themselves and in memory of the one who has died, they are able to feel hope that their lives can assume new meaning and strength. For the Christian, hope is expressed both for the loved one who has died and for the grieving person who affirms that God will never forsake him.

*Readjustment to life.* There is a real struggle to readjust to reality and to form new relationships in life. Even after time has been allowed for us to work through the various preceding stages of grief, this step does not come easily. However, we can recognize that healing involves not only the readiness to grieve but also the courage to begin again our involvement with life. Rather than giving in to self-pity, we can nudge ourselves into going on with the business of living. Actually it is somewhat idolatrous if we say or feel that we love the lost one so much that we cannot go on living without him. We imply that our love for a person is greater than our love for God! In essence this final step is the psychological death, burial, and resurrection. We move back into life, though we still carry the wounds of grief indefinitely.

## TELLING A CHILD ABOUT DEATH

Many children have been denied the opportunity to grieve normally because they were not dealt with honestly concerning the death of a loved one. One study indicated that children who have not been assisted in expressing their grief verbally do so through actions. Numerous studies revealed behavioral problems in children and youth who had experienced the death of a parent when they were younger.[6] For a more detailed study in child bereavement, see Erna Furman's *A Child's Parent Dies.*[7]

Much of the difficulty adults have in dealing with or talking about their grief stems from their childhood experiences with death. A minister has a significant role here for his parishoners—both for the adults who have hang-ups and for the young who will have them unless they receive assistance. We need to encourage parents to talk about death when it is a part of their child's experience. In understanding their child's feelings, parents need to be open and honest. This can be done within a better frame of reference if parents do not wait until a family member dies. Instead, they can talk naturally in response to children who ask about the dead bird, what a cemetery is, or why grandparents cannot run and play like children.

All adults need to be careful not to describe tragedy or death as God's will, or a child will lose a sense of trust in God and see him only as an evil God of death. This is especially true if a child is told the superficial lie that God took the loved one because he wanted him to come live with him. The Bible says that it is not God's will that any should suffer. Though he allows suffering as part of our human fabric, God does not desire it for us.

Children also need to be spared concepts such as one prayer, which states: ". . . if I should die before I wake. . . ." A child will develop a real anxiety about going to sleep when it seems to be equated with death. Likewise, parents should not use expressions such as: "Oh, you just kill me!" If the parent died of a heart attack the night after making such a statement, the child would always hold itself responsible for the death.

Fear about death can grow in children, but so can confidence that life is not all fearful or bad. Honest, direct dealing about death can help them to develop the ability to understand and relate both to their own deaths and to intense personal grief. Also, by learning that death is natural for the aged but unnatural for youth, children can learn to use caution and to value good health.

It is important to deal with children where they are, to answer just the questions they are asking. Due to age and temperament, not all children want to know the same things at the same time. It is interesting to observe that adults can help themselves when dealing honestly with children about death. In essence, adults may complete some unfinished feelings from their own childhoods about death!

Children need not be overprotected. They need to be able to talk comfortably about death just as they need to be allowed to work through their own griefs. Refusal to talk about death with children creates a silent vacuum that is filled with anxiety and curiosity. A lot of discussion is taking places in high schools and colleges about death. A teen-ager in my church said his favorite subject this past semester was the one on death. I teach about death in a public course offered at night by a local college. I feel that a minister should lead in helping his people to realize that the church and the home should not be silent about death and grief. Just as parents do not want some unknown teacher to teach their children about religion, so ministers should help parents to have the insight and courage to become the best possible source of reference in their children's quest for understanding about death and grief.

## Some Practical Suggestions

A minister can do a great service for bereaved church members when he can show them that their minister feels that honest grief is good. We can help members even more when we affirm that honest grief may open the way to God, to ourselves, and to the whole process of healing. Because the role of the minister is crucial in the experience of death and grief, it is important for him to consider the significance of postfuneral counseling. Everything that has been written thus far in this chapter will not mean anything unless a minister is willing to add it to his storehouse of knowledge and understanding and then relate to people who ache with grief. Some counselors say that the grief process takes a minimum of six months and six to ten hours of discussing the loss with a caring, nonjudgmental listener. I am suggesting some important things to bear in mind as a minister when you relate to grieving persons.

**Recognize and verbalize the impact of death and grief.** A minister will not provide help to a grieving family when he does not acknowledge the finality death places on physical life. There are too many platitudes uttered by insensitive ministers who have not tapped the roots of their own feelings. What good is it to a young widow with several children to rear when a minister says glibly to her about her dead husband: "Well, we know he'll be better off where he is."? How can a young couple be comforted at the death of their child when a minister says: "The Lord giveth and the Lord taketh away—blessed be the name of the Lord."?

I fear that, as a profession, ministers have developed one of the most unique camouflages for themselves. They have the inroad to a holy language that, for the most part, has been unquestioned by the general populace. I stood in the funeral home beside a widow whose husband had been tragically killed. Her very being ached because of how this disaster had torn her life apart. One young minister from the community came by and, with a big smile on his appeasing face, shook her hand. As he did so, he merrily said: "I know your faith will see you through." Somewhat shocked by this empty, naïve declaration, the grieving widow managed to utter: "I am not sure if I have any faith right now." The now-disarmed minister hurriedly said as he pulled away from her to leave: "Oh, now, you mustn't talk like that! Why I know your great Christian faith will stand up just fine!" Not once did he display any concern for her as a person. Never did he acknowledge that he even recognized the impact of death and grief. What he did do was convey that he would shield himself from any and all of her hurt with his holy language.

**Use Edgar N. Jackson's book, You and Your Grief.** I have found that one of the best ways of opening up in-depth conversation about how bereaved persons feel is to give the family a copy of this book. Obviously, for the minister who has never read it, he would want to be familiar with this book before giving it. As a matter of fact, a close study of the book will facilitate a minister's understanding of what a grieving family is experiencing. The book is brief and easy to read. It is inexpensive to give to church members who have experienced a death in their immediate family. Or copies from the church library might be loaned to these families.

I usually give the family the book on my first contact with them several days after the funeral. I follow up a couple of weeks later and ask them how things are going with them. If they do not mention it first, I ask them how they felt when they read the book. Most often I get a spontaneous response as to how helpful it has been. At that point I encourage them to talk about their feelings, to be open and honest about their grief. I acknowledge my awareness of the state of shock they have been in, and I give them assurance that it is good for them to express their emotions. Almost without fail people will apologize for any crying they do. How sad it is that we have made people feel embarrassed about expressing their feelings!

Often the bereaved will describe other feelings they are having. Either as reinforcement of what they have expressed or as prediction of what they might experience, I urge them to feel comfortable in talking about their depression, guilt, hostility, loneliness, fear, anxiety, and inability to function. Most often people seem relieved to hear me say that these are normal reactions, especially of Christians.

**Be honest with the bereaved.** I feel a most important aspect of grief counseling is basic honesty on the part of the minister. If you try to be the master healer, or if you are naive and glib, you will undermine your effectiveness. People know you are human. They can rather quickly tune out your pious God-talk and recognize that you do not understand or deeply care for them.

Do not attempt to make people retreat from death and grief. Acknowledge their loss and then seek to help them cope with it. Certainly refrain from making promises that time will heal all wounds. It is a long difficult task to become reoriented to life. Even then life will never be fully the same as it was before the death of a close loved one. At the same time I do not say that life has no meaning until we die and are united with the loved one and with Christ. Death is not the end of the loved one in Christ, and their death does not terminate all meaning for them in our lives.

**Help those in grief to recognize God's presence.** A special aid for those who mourn is the reassurance that God still loves and cares for them. In the midst of their hostility and anger toward God, they may arouse some feelings of guilt in themselves. In either case, they may need some genuine reaffirmation that while God allows us to be human—to suffer, to die, and to grieve—he never forsakes us. For those who are in Christ, the love of God as revealed in the Resurrection holds hope for us all. We can remind grieving persons that God has said we are not to "grieve as others do who have no hope." (1 Thess. 4:13b.)

I find it helpful to spend some time talking about the meaning and importance of prayer. If mourners understand how to pray and what to pray for, the utilization of prayer can be of great assistance in coming to grips with grief. It means a great deal for people to realize that it is good for them to express their feelings before God—their confession as well as their petition for strength and purpose in life. It is comforting for them to know that prayer is more than words uttered. At times when they seek to commune with God, he perceives their feelings even when they are quiet, when they are crying, or when they are meditating. Indeed, the Spirit intercedes for us when we are so burdened we do not know how or cannot utter words.

**Establish a Grief Growth Group.** I know that until I had been through my own grief after the death of a close family member, I did not really understand what a person in grief experiences. Since that time I have been much more perceptive and empathetic than I possibly could have been previously.

I feel grief is a point where the church can exercise itself as a community of love and concern. There is sharing and undergirding that Christians can offer one other and thereby facilitate the process of grief. One form of doing this was suggested in a lecture by Dr. Howard J. Clinebell. His approach is to have a group experience for those in the church who have recently faced grief. While focusing primarily on death, he conceives of grief in the broader dimension described earlier in this chapter.

Using the minister or some other trained person as a facilitator of the group, he suggests that each person sitting in the group, limited in size to no more than ten, share his loss with the others. After everyone in the group has actively listened to each one's deepest hurt, they are one by one to express a reaction in words or action toward the one who has just spoken. As each person shares his grief, the others in the group make their response. I have witnessed that the experiences in this group do a great deal toward healing grief and giving strength to face life once again.

A church could have a Grief Growth Group meet

periodically, allowing those still in grief to repeat, while adding those who are newly experiencing grief. For many this will be the strongest means of love and nurturing they will experience during their grief. For others the very act of hearing group members describe their grief will enable them to get in touch with and to verbalize their own grief.

**Teach the church to minister in grief.** In addition to the Grief Growth Group concept, a minister can enlarge his ministry by training the membership to minister the grief of others. Friends can help others to find the courage and hope to go on again. But this will not be the case if, by the time the funeral flowers have died, all of their friends cease visiting them.

I feel two of the most helpful things church members can do are to keep in contact with the bereaved family and to mention the dead person by name. All too often the close group of couples now exclude the new widow for fear she will be uncomfortable around them without her husband. Children with only one parent will miss the fishing trips and camp-outs. This need not be the case. After the death of a member of the family, there is even more need for the caring Christian community—close friends and new friends alike—to include both individual members and the entire family in group plans. Companionship and fellowship are big contributors to the process of working through grief in a normal fashion.

I have heard people say that they feel uncomfortable mentioning a dead person to the family for fear of bringing up sad emotions. There is no truth in such a notion. The reason we do not want to talk about the person may be due to our own fear of death or our unresolved feelings toward grief. It is only as we allow people to talk about, cry about, laugh about their dead loved one that we help to give them the ability and opportunity to work through their grief.

I have initiated a final facet of the church's ministry by training deacons to have a follow-up ministry with the bereaved. On an assignment basis, deacons visit families who are still working through the grief process. I receive reports from them and am referred to people who might need additional attention from me.

**Let people know their minister cares about them.** There is no set formula for the manner in which a minister reveals his love and care for his members. But they know whether or not you care. If they feel you take their hurt and loss seriously, they will feel comfortable in relating to you, both in counseling and in informal settings. They will feel particularly strengthened when they sense you are open to continuing to minister to their attempts to adjust to their loss and to cope with their grief.

Through your perception you can determine, after the two or three contacts following the funeral, whether to continue counseling on a regular basis. Due to the size of congregations, not every minister can maintain regular sessions with a large number of people. But almost everyone can continue to minister to those who appear to be having severe problems, even if the follow-up involves another staff member or an outside trained counselor. Nearly every minister could provide for a loving, listening experience such as a Grief Growth Group. And even if a personal encounter cannot be initiated, at least a note could be sent or a telephone call made on the anniversary of the death to families who have experienced grief. This act indicates continued caring and opens the way for the family to feel comfortable in asking for additional assistance in the process of interpreting and dealing with their grief.

At some point in his life everyone is acquainted with grief. Honest grief is good. It can be a means of opening us up to ourselves and to God. The role of the minister in grief is a crucially important one. The minister who is in touch with himself can feel along with and enter into the grief others are experiencing. The one who would minister to others can best do so when he has interpreted his own expectation of his religion and determined his own vision of God in time of trouble.

Dr. Claypool set the needs of everyone in proper perspective when he wrote of the crises with his daughter.[8] People who have false expectations of their religion will only be disappointed and disillusioned when they hit the bottom in a crisis. Those who see God as the panacea for all personal ills are ripe for hostility against God. In her evaluation of the strength of religion, Dr. Kübler-Ross has indicted minister and parishioner alike, whether we are facing death or grief. She said a little bit of religion is worse than no religion at all. A shallow concept of and relationship to God is more of a detriment than an aid.

When a minister comes to grips with his own feelings about life and death, he can help his parishioners relate more realistically to the vital issues of dying, death, and grief. And, in the long run, this may be one of the most significant aspects of his work a minister will ever perform. .

# 8
# Suggested Resources for Funerals

## INTRODUCTION

From its inception, this book was not intended to be a funeral manual. For this reason there is no attempt to include all the materials for a funeral service. My goal is to make a minister aware of the resources of his Bible, his hymnal, and himself to deal adequately with a funeral and with grief counseling. As you examine the lists on the following pages, you will be able to see some of the vast reservoirs of strength available from God's Word and the heritage of the Christian faith.

## ORDER OF WORSHIP

I feel very strongly that a funeral is an experience of corporate worship of God. Therefore I find it both important and appropriate to have a specific order of worship. When it is desired by the family to have congregational singing, I always have a printed order of worship. At all times the musicians, funeral director, and I have an order of worship. The following is a sample, one that is quite flexible at several points:

> Sacred Organ Music
> Opening Sentence
> Hymn
> Invocation
> Hymn (or anthem)
> Old Testament Lesson
> Prayer
> Anthem (or hymn or organ meditation)
> New Testament Lesson
> Meditation
> Hymn (or Organ Postlude could follow Benediction)
> Benediction (spoken and/or choral)
> Organ·Postlude
> Graveside Rites

## Opening Sentences

The following passages are appropriate for reading at the beginning of the funeral.

> Deut. 33:27a
> Josh. 1:6, 9
> Ps. 25:1, 16–18
>  27:1, 11, 14
>  31:24
>  46:10–11
>  55:22
>  86:3–5
>  91:1–2
>  103:11, 13–14

121:1–2
124:8
145:18
147:1–3
Isa. 41:10 or 10, 13
    43:1–3a
    54:10
Nah. 1:7
Matt. 5:4
    11:28–30
1 Cor. 2:9
2 Cor. 12:9

## HYMNS

The following is a list of some of the great hymns of the Church. These would be helpful for the worshipping community, either to be played or sung:

"A Mighty Fortress Is Our God"
"Abide With Me"
"Amazing Grace"
"Beneath the Cross of Jesus"
"Blessed Assurance"
"Christ the Lord Is Risen Today"
"Come, Thou Almighty King"
"Come, Thou Fount of Every Blessing"
"Crown Him with Many Crowns"
"Dear Lord and Father of Mankind"
"Eternal Father, Strong to Save"
"God So Loved the World"
"Great Is Thy Faithfulness"
"Guide Me, O Thou Great Jehovah"

"How Firm a Foundation"
"I Heard the Voice of Jesus Say"
"I Know That My Redeemer Liveth"
"I Need Thee Every Hour"
"It Is Well with My Soul"
"Jesus, Lover of My Soul"
"Jesus, Saviour, Pilot Me"
"Lead, Kindly Light"
"Lead On, O King Eternal"
"Leave It There"
"Love Divine, All Loves Excelling"
"My Faith Looks Up to Thee"
"Nearer My God to Thee"
"Now Thank We All Our God"
"Now the Day Is Over"
"O God, Our Help in Ages Past"
"O Love That Wilt Not Let Me Go"
"O Master, Let Me Walk with Thee"
"O Sacred Head, Now Wounded"
"Oh Jesus I Have Promised"
"Our Father, Who Art in Heaven"
"Rock of Ages"
"Saviour, Like a Shepherd Lead Us"
"Ten Thousand Times Ten Thousand"
"The Church's One Foundation"
"The King of Love My Shepherd Is"
"The Lord's My Shepherd, I'll Not Want"
"There Is a Balm in Gilead"
"There's a Wideness in God's Mercy"
"To God Be the Glory"
"What a Friend We Have in Jesus"
"When I Survey the Wondrous Cross"

If the training and availability of a choir permit, anthems might be used. The themes or texts might come from those similar to the suggested hymns. Other examples might include from Handel's Messiah, "I Know That My Redeemer Liveth," or J. Stainer's "God So Loved the World." If solos are used, encouragement can be given to avoid sentimental hymns in favor of great hymns of the Christian faith. In addition to the hymn texts, which might be used as solos, other possibilities would be "Come Unto Him," or "He Shall Feed His Flock" from the Messiah.

## Scripture

I have discovered that the Word of God can say far more to the bereaved family than any words of mine. For this reason I spend a great deal of time and consideration in attempting to select appropriate Scripture. Also, the amount of time spent reading from the Bible exceeds the time devoted to the funeral meditation.

Some funeral manuals have arbitrarily placed various passages into certain categories. While this was a possible way for me to list some significant Scripture, I felt it would be more helpful to encourage you to familiarize yourself with the broad scope of Scripture and determine your own categories. On the one hand, this is not a funeral manual. And on the other hand, one passage might be helpful to use in several different types of funerals.

*1. Old Testament Lessons*
    2 Sam. 12:16–23
    Ps.     1
          15
          16
          23
          27:1, 7–11, 13–14
          39:4–13
          46

Ps.   73:24–26, 28
91:1–4
103:1–5, 11–18
119:9–16
121
139:1–14, 23–24
Prov. 31:10–12, 20, 10–31
Isa. 35:3–10
40:1–11, 28–31
43:1–3a

*2. New Testament Lessons*
Matt. 5:3–12
6:19–21, 33
9:18–26
10:29–31
11:28–30
18:1–6
19:14
Mark 5:22–43 or 22–24, 35–43
Luke 7:11–15
11:9–13
John 10:7–18
11:11–26
14:1–11, 15–18, 26–28
Rom. 8:1–28
8:31–39
14:7–9
15:12, 17, 19–22
1 Cor. 15:35–38, 42–44, 49, 54–58
2 Cor. 1:3–7
4:5–18
5:1–10
Eph. 6:10–18a
Phil. 1:21

Phil. 2:5–11
    3:7–16
    4:4–9, 13, 19
    4:11b–13
1 Thess. 5:1–11, 23–24
2 Tim. 4:6–8
Titus 2:11–14
1 Pet. 1:3–9
    2:1–10
    2:19–25
2 Pet. 3:8–14
1 John 2:12–17
    4:7–21
Rev. 7:13–17

## BENEDICTION

I have not intended to collect a whole series of prayers and benedictions for funeral usage. However, I am indicating some appropriate biblical benedictions:

Num. 6:24–26
Rom. 15:13
1 Cor. 1:3
2 Cor. 13:14
Phil. 4:7
    4:19–20
1 Thess. 5:23
2 Thess. 2:16–17
1 Tim. 1:17
Heb. 13:20–21
1 Pet. 5:10b–11
Jude 24–25
Rev. 1:5b–6

## CHORAL BENEDICTIONS

Some examples of helpful choral benedictions include the following:

"Blest Be the Tie"
"God Be with You"
"Hallelujah Chorus" from *Messiah*
"The Heavens Declare His Glory"

## GRAVESIDE SCRIPTURE

I have found three passages to be very much to the point of that hour. They are:

Job 19:25–27
John 11:17–26
2 Cor. 4:17–18

## COMMITTAL

For a Christian, I suggest the following committal:

Cherishing memories that are forever sacred;
Sustained by a faith that is stronger than death;
Comforted by the hope of a life that shall endless be;
We commit to the earth all that is mortal of this our friend.
As we have born the image of the earthy,
So shall we also bear the image of the heavenly.[1]

In the case of cremation or willing of the body to medical science, the committal might read:

Cherishing memories that are forever sacred;
Sustained by a faith that is stronger than death;
Comforted by the hope of a life that shall endless be;
We acknowledge the death of this our friend.
As we have born the image of the earthy,
So shall we also bear the image of the heavenly.

If the person being buried was not a professing Christian, the following committal would be appropriate:

Cherishing memories that are forever sacred;
Sustained by a faith that is stronger than death;
Comforted by the hope of a life that shall endless be;
We commit to the earth all that is mortal of this our friend.
We leave the future in the hands of our God,
The Creator of all things,
Who in his boundless mercy, almighty power, and infinite understanding will do all things well.

## GRAVESIDE BENEDICTION

The biblical benedictions listed earlier might be well used at this point. Heb. 13:20–21 seems particularly appropriate. I also like, and most often use, the prayer of John Henry Newman:

O Lord, support us all the day long of our troublous life,
until the shadows lengthen
and the evening comes,
and the busy world is hushed,
and the fever of life is over,

and our work is done.
Then in thy mercy grant us a safe lodging
and a holy rest,
and peace at the last,
through Jesus Christ our Lord.
Amen.[2]

# Conclusion

It is now obvious to the reader that this book is not a tool to be carried to the pulpit for a funeral. However, I do hope that at least four things have been accomplished through this book:

1. Every minister needs to recognize that he cannot help his parishioners deal therapeutically with grief until he has come to grips with the reality of his own death. Often when a person experiences an intense grief himself he is open to face his own life and death with deeper seriousness. If a minister is unable to face the reality of his own humanness through his own strengths and insights, he can avail himself of professional assistance.

2. The average church member longs to hear a Word from God through his spokesman that will help develop a reservoir of strength to live life fully and face death courageously. Surely sermons on the topic of death and grief should receive as high a priority as the perennial sermons that seek to help underwrite the church's budget. No minister should ask a member to draw from a well of faith, confidence, and hope when the minister has not helped to establish that resource.

3. Each death is unique in itself. A minister should not expect to relate to two grief situations in the same way. At the

same time there are some positive courses of action a minister can determine to follow in advance, so that a healthy reaction to grief can be effected.

4. The Bible, the hymnal, and one's own positive outlook on life and death provide innumerable responses for aiding a bereaved family. Familiarity with the resources can enable a minister to relate more meaningfully to the needs of a specific family. The examples given were meant to be neither the only response nor a stereotyped reaction. They represent simply one course of action in one hypothetical situation.

By the grace of God and with thoughtful evaluation and careful preparation, every minister can more adequately fill his priestly role at the time of death. Be open to all of God's good gifts to you so that you can reach your highest capabilities in his name.

# Appendix

THE WORSHIP OF GOD
At the Funeral of Mr. Samuel S. Smith[1]
March 20, 1970

SACRED ORGAN MUSIC "A Mighty Fortress Is Our God"

OPENING SENTENCES

The Lord is my light and my salvation;
whom shall I fear?
the Lord is the strength of my life;
of whom shall I be afraid?
Teach me thy way, O Lord,
and lead me in a plain path, because of mine enemies.
Wait on the Lord:
be of good courage, and he shall strengthen thine heart:
wait, I say, on the Lord (Ps. 27:1, 11, 14 AV)

Hymn No. 286: "O God, Our Help in Ages Past"

O God, our help in ages past,
Our hope for years to come,
Our shelter from the stormy blast,
And our eternal home!

Under the shadow of thy throne
Thy saints have dwelt secure;
Sufficient is thine arm alone,
And our defense is sure.

Before the hills in order stood,
Or earth received her frame,
From everlasting thou art God,
To endless years the same.

A thousand ages in thy sight
Are like an evening gone;
Short as the watch that ends the night
Before the rising sun.

O God, our help in ages past,
Our hope for years to come,
Be thou our guard while life shall last,
And our eternal home.[2]

### INVOCATION

O God, at all times when we seek thee do we find
strength and meaning. We ask that thou would make
thyself known to each person in this hour. While we
cannot fathom fully the mysteries of life and death,
enable us to be encountered and uplifted by thy presence,

thy love, thy comfort, and thy strength. In Jesus' name we pray. Amen.

## Old Testament Lesson

Frequently there are times in our lives when we long so desperately to hear some Word from the Lord, to gain some insight and meaning for our experience. Hear him now as he speaks through his Word. Though written centuries ago, he has a fresh and vital Word for this day. God spoke through the psalmist, saying:

> God is our refuge and strength, a very present help in trouble. Therefore will not we fear, though the earth be removed, and though the mountains be carried into the midst of the sea; Be still, and know that I am God: I will be exalted among the heathen, I will be exalted in the earth. The Lord of hosts is with us; the God of Jacob is our refuge. (Ps. 46:1–3, 10–11 AV)

The prophet Isaiah recorded these words to the Hebrew people in Babylonian captivity, far from their homes. Hear this Word that speaks comfort and hope to us today:

> Hast thou not known? hast thou not heard, that the everlasting God, the Lord, the Creator of the ends of the earth, fainteth not, neither is weary? There is no searching of his understanding. He giveth power to the faint; and to them that have no might he increaseth strength. Even the youths shall faint and be weary, and the young men shall utterly fall: But they that wait upon the Lord shall renew their strength; they shall mount up with wings as eagles; they shall run, and not be weary; and they shall walk, and not faint. (Isa. 40:28–31 AV)

The psalmist wrote words of meaning and comfort to all anxious persons in the most familiar of all the Psalms:

The Lord is my shepherd; I shall not want. He maketh me to lie down in green pastures: he leadeth me beside the still waters. He restoreth my soul: he leadeth me in the paths of righteousness for his name's sake. Yea, though I walk through the valley of the shadow of death, I will fear no evil: for thou art with me; thy rod and thy staff they comfort me. Thou preparest a table before me in the presence of mine enemies: thou annointest my head with oil; my cup runneth over. Surely goodness and mercy shall follow me all the days of my life: and I will dwell in the house of the Lord for ever. (Ps. 23 AV)

### PRAYER

O Father of mercies and God of all comfort, who dost comfort us in all our affliction, deal graciously with thy servants who mourn, that as they cast all their care upon thee they may know the strength and consolation of thy love.

Remind us that thou art the giver of all good gifts, and that thou dost not give as the world giveth. For what thou giveth thou takest not away, for what is thine is ours always, if we are thine. And life in thee is eternal!

Lift us up, therefore, strong Son of God, that we may see beyond the darkness of this hour. Cleanse our eyes from the tears of grief that we may behold thee more clearly. Draw us closer to thyself that we may know ourselves nearer to our beloved Christian brother who is with thee.

While thou dost prepare a place for us, prepare us both

for that place and for living each day with thee, so that where thou art, there we may be too. Grant us steadfast faith and sure hope in thou who art the Resurrection and the Life, in whose name we pray.         Amen.

ORGAN MEDITATION "Beneath the Cross of Jesus"

NEW TESTAMENT LESSON

May we continue to hear God speak to us through his word recorded in the New Testament. The apostle Paul wrote:

What shall we then say to these things? If God be for us, who can be against us? He that spared not his own Son, but delivered him up for us all, how shall he not with him also freely give us all things? Who shall lay any thing to the charge of God's elect? It is God that justifieth. Who is he that condemneth? It is Christ that died, yea rather, that is risen again, who is even at the right hand of God, who also maketh intercession for us. Who shall separate us from the love of Christ? Shall tribulation, or distress, or persecution, or famine, or nakedness, or peril, or sword? As it is written, For thy sake we are killed all the day long; we are accounted as sheep for the slaughter. Nay, in all these things we are more than conquerors through him that loved us. For I am persuaded, that neither death, nor life, nor angels, nor principalities, nor powers, nor things present, nor things to come, nor height, nor depth, nor any other creature, shall be able to separate us from the love of God, which is in Christ Jesus our Lord (Rom. 8:31-39 AV)

Paul also wrote:

For none of us liveth to himself, and no man dieth to himself. For whether we live, we live unto the Lord; and whether we die, we die unto the Lord: whether we live therefore, or die, we are the Lord's. For to this end Christ both died, and rose, and revived, that he might be Lord both of the dead and of the living. (Rom. 14:7–9 AV)

To his troubled disciples Jesus spoke these words:

Let not your heart be troubled: ye believe in God, believe also in me. In my Father's house are many mansions: if it were not so, I would have told you. I go to prepare a place for you. And if I go and prepare a place for you, I will come again, and receive you unto myself; that where I am, there ye may be also. And whither I go ye know, and the way ye know. Thomas saith unto him, Lord, we know not whither thou goest; and how can we know the way? Jesus saith unto him, I am the way, the truth, and the life: no man cometh unto the Father but by me. If ye had known me, ye should have known my Father also: and from henceforth ye know him, and have seen him. Philip saith unto him, Lord, show us the Father, and it sufficeth us. Jesus saith unto him, Have I been so long time with you, and yet hast thou not known me, Philip? He that hath seen me hath seen the Father; and how sayest thou then, Show us the Father?

Peace I leave with you, my peace I give unto you: not as the world giveth, give I unto you. Let not your heart be troubled, neither let it be afraid. Ye have heard how I said unto you, I go away, and come again unto you. If ye loved me, ye would rejoice, because I said, I go unto the Father; for my Father is greater than I. (John 14:1–9, 27–28 AV)

A Word that seems so contemporary to his followers of every generation was expressed by Jesus when he said:

Come unto me, all ye that labour and are heavy laden, and I will give you rest. Take my yoke upon you, and learn of me; for I am meek and lowly in heart: and ye shall find rest unto your souls. For my yoke is easy, and my burden is light. (Matt. 11:28–30 AV)

## MEDITATION

The whole world is bursting forth in spring today! The one who calls us to this hour was one who thoroughly enjoyed all the beauty of God's world. He loved to work in the ground and see things grow. Of all people he might understand the mystery of life and death. He knew that what appeared to be dead under the ground was really alive and preparing to bring forth new life.

Grief is always hard to deal with, but never is it more difficult than when death comes suddenly and unexpectedly. Since he was loved, his absence will hurt even more deeply.

Yet I am not ashamed to stand before this family and offer them the assurance that even now God does not forsake us. While our bodies are made of clay and do not last forever, our relationship begun with God does sustain us through every kind of experience in this life and finally will bring us into a full relationship with God beyond this life.

God offers through his Spirit and through fellow Christians the love, peace, comfort, hope, and courage for you to go on living without one who has meant so much to his wife, daughter, brothers and sisters, and a host of friends. Do not be ashamed of your grief, but know that you are not alone. Not only do friends stand by you, but also God is with you now and forevermore.

Now you must begin to make adjustments to live without this loved one. May you recognize the presence and companionship of God in Christ who will give you the peace that passeth all understanding—for this and every day of your life. Then you can find the joy and meaning of living. And you can know the beauty God intended for your life as you daily come to full bloom.

May God give you the strength so to live today and every day.

### BENEDICTION

Almighty God, we come to thee because we need thee. Without thee we are poor and weak, and with thee we can find the wealth of thy strength for the living of these hours.

We bow ourselves before thee and ask that thou would guide us through an experience filled with darkness, grief, and stress. Bring thy comfort to these hearts that are heavy with sorrow. May they be especially aware of thy divine presence. Remind them also of the strength in the love, prayers, and presence of their Christian friends.

Father, send us all back to our lives more eager to serve thee, and more inclined to love thee, as though in this mysterious presence here we have learned to know the deeper meaning and responsibility of life. In the midst of all the changes of this world, make us strong and calm, because we rest in thee and know that nothing—even death—can separate us from thy love in Christ Jesus Our Lord, in whose name we pray.     Amen.

## GRAVESIDE RITES

*Scripture.*     Then Martha, as soon as she heard that Jesus was coming, went and met him: but Mary sat still in the house. Then said Martha unto Jesus, Lord, if thou hadst been here, my brother had not died. But I know, that even now, whatsoever thou wilt ask of God, God will give it thee. Jesus saith unto her, thy brother shall rise again. Martha said unto him, I know that he shall rise again in the resurrection at the last day. Jesus saith unto her, I am the resurrection and the life: he that believeth in me, though he were dead, yet shall he live: and whosoever liveth and believeth in me shall never die. Believest thou this? (John 11:20–26 AV)

*Committal.*     Cherishing memories that are forever sacred;
Sustained by a faith that is stronger than death;
Comforted by the hope of a life that shall endless be;
We commit to the earth all that is mortal of this our friend.
As we have born the image of the earthy,
So shall we also bear the image of the heavenly.[3]

*Benediction.*     O, Lord, support us all the day long of our troublous life, until the shadows lengthen and the evening comes, and the busy world is hushed, and the fever of life is over, and our work is done. Then in thy mercy grant us a safe lodging and a holy rest, and peace at the last, through Jesus Christ our Lord.     Amen.[4]

# Notes

CHAPTER 1

1. Helmut Thielicke, *Death and Life*, trans. Edward H. Schroeder (Philadelphia: Fortress Press, 1970), p. 7.
2. Edgar N. Jackson, *Telling A Child About Death* (New York: Hawthorn Books, 1965), p. 90.
3. George Benson, "Death and Dying: A Psychoanalytic Perspective," *The Journal of Pastoral Care*, June 1972, p. 80.
4. "Is That All There Is?" Words and music by Terry Leiber and Mike Stoller, © 1966, Yellow Dog Music, Inc.
5. From C. S. Lewis, *A Grief Observed*, © 1961 by N. W. Clerk. Used by permission of The Seabury Press, Inc., p. 47ff.
6. John R. Claypool, *Tracks of a Fellow Struggler* (Waco, Tex.: Word Books, 1974), p. 75.
7. Frederick Buechner, *Wishful Thinking* (New York: Harper & Row, 1973), p. 47.
8. Claypool, *Tracks of a Fellow Struggler*, p. 57ff.
9. Virginia Satir, *Peoplemaking* (Palo Alto, Calif.: Science and Behavior Books, 1972), p. 250.
10. From William Stringfellow, *Instead of Death* (New York: © by The Seabury Press, Inc. 1963), p. 11. Used by permission.
11. Jackson, *Telling a Child About Death*, pp. 90–91.
12. Stephen Vincent Benét, "A Child Is Born," in *We Stand United and Other Radio Scripts*, (New York: Rinehart & Company, Copyright 1942 by Stephen Vincent Benét.) Reprinted by permission of Brandt & Brandt.
13. Leonard Griffith, *God in Man's Experience* (Waco, Tex.: Word Books, 1968), p. 37.

CHAPTER 2

1. Elizabeth Kübler-Ross, *On Death and Dying* (New York: Macmillan Co., 1969).
2. Elton Trueblood, *The Common Ventures of Life* (New York: Harper & Row, 1949), pp. 106–107.
3. Kübler-Ross, *On Death and Dying*, p. 254.
4. C. Charles Bachmann, *Ministering to the Grief Sufferer* (Philadelphia: Fortress Press, 1964), pp. 121ff.


CHAPTER 3

1. Lewis, *A Grief Observed*, p. 14.
2. Kübler-Ross, *On Death and Dying*, pp. 38–137.
3. Hugh Hamilton, "Death," *The Encyclopedia of Religious Quotations*, edited by Frank S. Mead (Westwood, N.J.: Fleming H. Revell Company, 1965), p. 101.
4. Joseph Bayly, *The View from a Hearse* (Elgin, Ill.: David C. Cook Publishing Co., 1973), p. 87.
5. William Shakespeare, *Julius Caesar*, act 2, scene 2, lines 28–29.
6. John Kelly, "Do the Dying Have the Right to Decide Their Fate?" *Family Weekly*, January 12, 1975, p. 6.


CHAPTER 6

1. Edgar N. Jackson, *You and Your Grief* (New York: Hawthorn Books, 1962).


CHAPTER 7

1. Bachmann, *Ministering to the Grief Sufferer*, pp. 127–129.
2. Paul Tournier, *The Meaning of Persons* (New York: Harper & Row, 1959), p. 219.
3. Granger E. Westberg, *Good Grief* (Philadelphia: Fortress Press, 1973).
4. David Bogard, *Valleys and Vistas* (Grand Rapids: Baker Book House, 1974).
5. Lewis, *A Grief Observed*, p. 7.
6. Jackson, *Telling a Child About Death*, pp. 16–18.
7. Erna Furman, *A Child's Parent Dies* (New Haven: Yale University Press, 1974).
8. Claypool, *Tracks of a Fellow Struggler*, p. 51ff.

## Notes

### CHAPTER 8

1. "Committal," *A Service Book* (Evanston, Ill.: National Selected Morticians, 1967), p. 49.
2. John Henry Newman, *A Service Book*, p. 90.


### APPENDIX

1. This is the funeral written for the fictitious case history described in chap. 6.
2. Isaac Watts, "O God, Our Help In Ages Past," written in 1719, based on Ps. 90:1-5.
3. "Committal," *A Service Book*, p. 49.
4. John Henry Newman, *A Service Book*, p. 90.